I0414285

AFGHANISTAN'S TERRORIST RESURGENCE: AL-QAEDA, ISIS, AND BEYOND

HEARING

BEFORE THE

SUBCOMMITTEE ON TERRORISM, NONPROLIFERATION, AND TRADE

OF THE

COMMITTEE ON FOREIGN AFFAIRS HOUSE OF REPRESENTATIVES

ONE HUNDRED FIFTEENTH CONGRESS

FIRST SESSION

APRIL 27, 2017

Serial No. 115–20

Printed for the use of the Committee on Foreign Affairs

Available via the World Wide Web: http://www.foreignaffairs.house.gov/ or http://www.gpo.gov/fdsys/

U.S. GOVERNMENT PUBLISHING OFFICE

25–262PDF WASHINGTON : 2017

For sale by the Superintendent of Documents, U.S. Government Publishing Office
Internet: bookstore.gpo.gov   Phone: toll free (866) 512–1800; DC area (202) 512–1800
Fax: (202) 512–2104   Mail: Stop IDCC, Washington, DC 20402–0001

COMMITTEE ON FOREIGN AFFAIRS

EDWARD R. ROYCE, California, *Chairman*

CHRISTOPHER H. SMITH, New Jersey
ILEANA ROS-LEHTINEN, Florida
DANA ROHRABACHER, California
STEVE CHABOT, Ohio
JOE WILSON, South Carolina
MICHAEL T. McCAUL, Texas
TED POE, Texas
DARRELL E. ISSA, California
TOM MARINO, Pennsylvania
JEFF DUNCAN, South Carolina
MO BROOKS, Alabama
PAUL COOK, California
SCOTT PERRY, Pennsylvania
RON DeSANTIS, Florida
MARK MEADOWS, North Carolina
TED S. YOHO, Florida
ADAM KINZINGER, Illinois
LEE M. ZELDIN, New York
DANIEL M. DONOVAN, JR., New York
F. JAMES SENSENBRENNER, JR.,
   Wisconsin
ANN WAGNER, Missouri
BRIAN J. MAST, Florida
FRANCIS ROONEY, Florida
BRIAN K. FITZPATRICK, Pennsylvania
THOMAS A. GARRETT, JR., Virginia

ELIOT L. ENGEL, New York
BRAD SHERMAN, California
GREGORY W. MEEKS, New York
ALBIO SIRES, New Jersey
GERALD E. CONNOLLY, Virginia
THEODORE E. DEUTCH, Florida
KAREN BASS, California
WILLIAM R. KEATING, Massachusetts
DAVID N. CICILLINE, Rhode Island
AMI BERA, California
LOIS FRANKEL, Florida
TULSI GABBARD, Hawaii
JOAQUIN CASTRO, Texas
ROBIN L. KELLY, Illinois
BRENDAN F. BOYLE, Pennsylvania
DINA TITUS, Nevada
NORMA J. TORRES, California
BRADLEY SCOTT SCHNEIDER, Illinois
THOMAS R. SUOZZI, New York
ADRIANO ESPAILLAT, New York
TED LIEU, California

AMY PORTER, *Chief of Staff*   THOMAS SHEEHY, *Staff Director*

JASON STEINBAUM, *Democratic Staff Director*

SUBCOMMITTEE ON TERRORISM, NONPROLIFERATION, AND TRADE

TED POE, Texas, *Chairman*

JOE WILSON, South Carolina
DARRELL E. ISSA, California
PAUL COOK, California
SCOTT PERRY, Pennsylvania
LEE M. ZELDIN, New York
BRIAN J. MAST, Florida
THOMAS A. GARRETT, JR., Virginia

WILLIAM R. KEATING, Massachusetts
LOIS FRANKEL, Florida
BRENDAN F. BOYLE, Pennsylvania
DINA TITUS, Nevada
NORMA J. TORRES, California
BRADLEY SCOTT SCHNEIDER, Illinois

CONTENTS

AFGHANISTAN'S TERRORIST RESURGENCE: AL-QAEDA, ISIS, AND BEYOND

THURSDAY, APRIL 27, 2017

House of Representatives,
Subcommittee on Terrorism, Nonproliferation, and Trade,
Committee on Foreign Affairs,
Washington, DC.

The subcommittee met, pursuant to notice, at 2:00 p.m., in room 2172 Rayburn House Office Building, Hon. Ted Poe (chairman of the subcommittee) presiding.

Mr. Poe. The subcommittee will come to order. Without objection, all members may have 5 days to submit statements, questions, and extraneous materials for the record subject to the length limitation and the rules. At this time, I am going to make my opening statement.

When our forces invaded Afghanistan in 2001, the goal was simple: Remove the Taliban government that sheltered the plotters of the 9/11 attacks and destroy al-Qaeda. It has been 16 years that the United States has been at war, and Afghanistan is still a haven for terrorists who seek to attack and kill Americans. Just today, two Americans were killed in the eastern province of Afghanistan. Our military quickly toppled the Taliban government in 2001, and the Taliban/al-Qaeda forces fled to Pakistan where they re- grouped and launched more attacks against our troops. Since then, the Taliban has waged insurgency in Afghanistan, destabilizing the country and creating perfect conditions for terrorists to exploit.

The Taliban insurgency today is stronger than any other point since 2001. The Special Inspector General for Afghan Reconstruction said in January, 171 Afghan districts are controlled, influenced, or contested by the Taliban. As long as the Taliban is successful this means good news for al-Qaeda. Al-Qaeda has a long history of loyalty to the Taliban, or Osama bin Laden swore allegiance to the Taliban's leader, Mullah Omar, even before 9/11. And when bin Laden was killed, Ayman al-Zawahiri renewed his oath that cemented ties between al-Qaeda and the Taliban. Wherever the Taliban has influenced, al-Qaeda is not behind.

Since 2010, United States' officials have claimed that al-Qaeda had a small presence in the country limited to only 50 to 100 fighters. That is absolutely incorrect. The United States has killed and captured more Afghan, more terrorists, since that time than was claimed to be in the entire country.

Alongside al-Qaeda and Afghanistan we have another terrorist group, the Haqqani Network. This group is directly linked to both al-Qaeda and the Taliban and is based, guess where, Pakistan. The Haqqani Network is responsible for more American deaths in the region than any other terrorist group. The Haqqani Network attacks inside Afghanistan have been directly traced back to Pakistan. In fact, in 2011, Admiral Mike Mullen, the chairman of the Joint Chiefs of Staff, testified before the Senate, "The Haqqani Network acts as a veritable arm of Pakistan's Inter-Services Intelligence agency."

It seems that Pakistan has ties to about every terrorist group that is in Afghanistan. Pakistan openly supported the Afghan Taliban both before and after the extremists took control of Kabul in 1996. We know the Taliban is still based in Pakistan, and it came to no surprise that when a U.S. drone strike killed the leader of the Taliban in May 2016, he was in southwestern Pakistan.

The laundry list of evidence of Pakistan support for terrorists goes on and on. We remember that when the al-Qaeda leader and America's most wanted terrorist, Osama bin Laden, was killed he was found in Pakistan. Afghan's representative to the U.N. recently told the Security Council that Pakistan retains ties with more than 20 terrorist groups. And I ask unanimous consent to introduce into the record the full statement made by Afghan's representative to the U.N. and it is admitted.

I believe Pakistan is playing us. They launched what they called counterterrorism operations in the tribal areas bordering Afghanistan, but it quickly became clear they were only targeting the Pakistani Taliban and not the Afghan Taliban.

ISIS announced the establishment of an Afghan affiliate in January 2013 and has entrenched itself in the eastern part of the country. ISIS presence in Afghan further complicates the country's terrorist landscape. These fighters ended up becoming the leaders of the ISIS affiliate in Afghanistan known as ISIS-Khorasan Province.

It is no surprise that Afghanistan is a mess. In the war on terror it is crystal clear to me that Pakistan is not on our side. It is time that we consider, one, listing Pakistanas a state sponsor of terrorism; two, stop sending them U.S. aid; three, remove and revoke their status as a major non-NATO U.S. ally. Our Pakistan policy should match Pakistan's behavior. And I will yield to the ranking member for his comments.

Mr. KEATING. Thank you, Chairman Poe. Two U.S. service members were killed in Afghanistan overnight. Reports indicate that they were killed in operations against Islamic State fighters in Nangarhar Province in eastern Afghanistan. Words are truly inadequate to express our country's gratitude at the extraordinary sacrifice of these individuals and heroes, and our prayers are with their families.

As the continued threat of insurgent groups and instability in the country poses a direct challenge to the United States, this year marks 16 years of military presence in Afghanistan following the September 11th attacks. Our own security is linked to Afghanistan's security, putting the elimination of terrorism there and putting them squarely within our interests, as well, as a country.

If we are to be successful in eradicating this threat, we must be sure that the U.S. strategy in Afghanistan is addressing the drivers of terrorism head on. Unfortunately, in Afghanistan, there are multiple drivers, and our prolonged military presence in the country underscores this complex reality.

Internally, Afghanistan's National Unity Government is still struggling to effectively address the many systemic problems facing their country. Organized crime, illicit economies, rampant corruption at all levels of the Afghan society require a coordinated and a robust approach from the government if Afghanistan is to achieve security from the national level all the way down to the community level.

Taliban control in Afghan communities impedes the government's ability to limit recruitment and the threat of terrorism throughout the country. Strengthening the role of a democratic Afghan Government at all levels is absolutely necessary in order to eradicate terrorism in the long term. Additionally, the Afghan military continues to encounter issues of internal accountability and operational effectiveness in combating terrorist groups.

I have witnessed U.S. military, along with our allied forces, training and advising Afghan forces for years and the significant progress they have made. However, there seem to be ongoing institutional challenges within the Afghan military that require further attention if their military is going to be sufficiently prepared to take on the long term responsibility of managing the terrorist threat in Afghanistan.

There is a role for the United States to play in ensuring that Afghanistan can achieve their own security and independently and internationally deal with the support necessary to do so. However, we also need to be clear on what form our role should take.

The security situation in Afghanistan, and by extension the United States, is multidimensional and not solely comprised of military objectives. The governance issues in Afghanistan that are stymied and that have stymied the progress in the fight against terrorism cannot be resolved solely through the use of force and integration of military expertise.

The whole of the government approach is what is necessary. That whole of the government approach that Afghanistan must take to combat this threat of terrorism should be complemented by the diverse expertise that the United States can offer in order to make sure the Afghan Government is most efficiently and effectively moving toward greater security within its own borders. This means ensuring that our State Department and other key government agencies have the capacity to engage meaningfully with their counterparts and partners in Afghanistan.

A whole of government approach here in the U.S. keeps our troops and allies safer. It also promotes longer stability in the country, a stability that will bring about a more rapid resolution to this conflict.

I, therefore, join many of my Democratic and Republican colleagues on and off the Foreign Affairs Committee who are deeply concerned about the proposed budget cuts to the State Department and the impact they would have on our objectives in the long term. This is not only because of the complex situation within Afghanistan, but because of the role that other countries play in exacerbating the terrorist threat inside the country.

We know that Iran and Russia have both provided assistance to the Taliban in an effort to counter the threat of the Islamic State groups in Afghanistan. Pakistan has had a long and complicated history and have long and complicated efforts to combat terrorism in Afghanistan through its acquiescence in providing safe haven to terrorists, particularly the Haqqanis.

So, we need a balanced approach to tackling the terrorist threat in Afghanistan that reflects the complex and dynamic reality on the ground and in the region. Why should we tie one hand behind our back when we have the experts ready and waiting to make this difficult process of eliminating terrorist threat, a process that should move forward more effectively and quickly, if we take this approach?

Today I am eager to hear from our witnesses about the lessons learned about what is working, what is not working, and why. This is important as the White House reassesses the U.S. strategy in Afghanistan and as Congress looks forward to an appropriations process which gives us the opportunity to make sure that the most effective strategies to bring peace and stability for Afghanistan and the United States are appropriately funded.

Thank you, Chairman Poe. I yield back.

Mr. POE. I thank the gentleman. So, without objection, all the witness' prepared statements will be made part of the record. I ask that each of the witnesses please keep your presentation to no more than 5 minutes, and when the red light comes on you need to stop or I will encourage you to stop. I will introduce each witness and then give them time for opening statements.

Mr. Bill Roggio—is it Roggio—is a Foundation for Defense of Democracies Senior Fellow and editor of the Long War Journal. Mr. Roggio was embedded with the U.S. Marines, the United States Army, and Iraqi forces in Iraq between 2005 and 2008, and with the Canadian Army in Afghanistan in 2006.

Dr. Seth Jones is director of the International Security and Defense Policy Center at the RAND Corporation. He previously served as the representative for the commander, U.S. Special Operations Command, to the Assistant Secretary of Defense for Special Operations.

And Dr. Vanda Felbab-Brown is a senior fellow in the Center for the 21st Century Security and Intelligence at the Brookings Institution. She is an expert on international and internal conflicts and nontraditional security threats.

Mr. Roggio, we will start with you. You have 5 minutes.

STATEMENT OF MR. BILL ROGGIO, EDITOR, LONG WAR JOURNAL, FOUNDATION FOR DEFENSE OF DEMOCRACIES

Mr. ROGGIO. Thank you, Chairman Poe and Ranking Member Keating, and the rest of the distinguished members of this committee. This is a timely discussion.

Last week the Taliban launched a major attack on an Afghan army base. Ten fighters launched what I call a suicide assault where the fighters penetrate security at the base, and they are not coming back. They are going to fight to the death. They killed at least 140 Afghan soldiers. This was an attack on an army corps base in northern Afghanistan, not in the south where everyone assumes the Taliban to be strong. I have seen reports of upwards of 250 Afghan troops killed in this attack.

The Taliban is using tactics that have been honed and perfected by al-Qaeda and now the Islamic State, which is the child of al-Qaeda. We are losing in Afghanistan. The U.S. military will tell you at best we are at a stalemate, but in a stalemate, in that situation, the tie goes to the insurgent and the Taliban controls or contests at least half of Afghanistan.

The Taliban issued a report in late March saying they control or contest 211 of Afghanistan's more than 400 districts. That is very close to the SIGAR report that you had mentioned where it was, I believe, 177. That assessment was given by SIGAR in the fall of 2016. In addition to—and the reason the Taliban matters is the Taliban and al-Qaeda, they remain tied at the hip. The Taliban refused to surrender al-Qaeda members and Osama bin Laden after the 9/11 attacks. They continue to fight side by side.

Al-Qaeda serves as a force multiplier. Multiple designations from the U.S. Treasury Department talk about how al-Qaeda and the Taliban fundraise for each other in the Gulf States. This includes the Haqqani Network by the way. And we continue to see al-Qaeda fighters killed on the battlefield. As a matter of fact, the U.S. military killed a senior al-Qaeda leader just last month inside Afghanistan.

So a lot has been made in the U.S. intelligence circles about the strength of al-Qaeda. Under the Obama administration, we were told there were 50 to 100 al-Qaeda fighters inside the country, and we were consistently given this estimate for more than 6 years. This all came crashing down in October 2015 when U.S. military raided two al-Qaeda camps; one of them described by a U.S. commander as possibly the largest al-Qaeda facility taken down since 9/11. This is in Afghanistan; not in Syria, not in Iraq, not in Somalia or Yemen. More than 150 al-Qaeda fighters were killed in this one raid alone. So, we basically took 150 percent of al-Qaeda's estimated strength by the U.S. military that was given in intelligence circles for more than 6 years.

We have an intelligence problem in Afghanistan. We have a problem recognizing what the threat is. Until we determine where al-Qaeda is inside Afghanistan and how they are working closely with the Taliban, we will continue to have a problem, and we will fail to properly deal with this threat. Today, a lot of the threat in Afghanistan is looked at as being the Islamic State's Khorasan Province. We dropped the mother of all bombs there, and as you both had mentioned, we lost two soldiers in Nangarhar Province last night.

The Islamic State is on the fringe. It is a small problem in Afghanistan compared to al-Qaeda, the Taliban, and other Pakistani jihadists groups that operate there. They operate primarily in four districts in Nangarhar Province and have a minimal presence in the north. It certainly is a problem. Our efforts seem to be focused on the Islamic State at this point in time while largely ignoring what the Taliban is doing throughout the country, and that is directly challenging the Afghan military. They are going toe to toe, they are raiding their bases, they are taking control of territory, and the U.S. military, frankly, has downplayed this problem with the Taliban.

When the Taliban overran the Sangin District, hundreds of U.S. Marines and British troops died trying to liberate it during the surge between 2010 and 2012. When the Taliban overran that district, the military put out—what I will say is—a ridiculous press release stating, no, no, the district wasn't overrun. We merely moved the district center, and the Taliban took control of rubble. And if that is the attitude of the U.S. military toward the Taliban inside Afghanistan, we will continue to lose this war.

We need to reassess Afghanistan. We need to—our policy in Afghanistan is a mess, frankly, and the Trump administration needs to decide what to do and how to do it, quickly. Thank you very much.

[The prepared statement of Mr. Roggio follows:]

CONGRESSIONAL TESTIMONY: FOUNDATION FOR DEFENSE OF DEMOCRACIES

House Foreign Affairs Committee, Subcommittee on Terrorism, Nonproliferation, and Trade

Afghanistan's Terrorist Resurgence:

Al-Qaeda, ISIS, and Beyond

BILL ROGGIO

Editor
FDD's Long War Journal

Senior Fellow
Foundation for Defense of Democracies

Washington, DC
April 27, 2017

www.defenddemocracy.org

Bill Roggio   April 27, 2017

Chairman Poe, Ranking Member Keating, and other members of this subcommittee, thank you for inviting me here today to speak about the terrorist groups based in Afghanistan and their continuing threat to U.S. national security.

More than 15 years after the U.S. military invaded Afghanistan to destroy al-Qaeda, the group maintains a persistent and significant presence in the country. Despite the Obama administration's surge of U.S. forces in Afghanistan from 2010 to 2012, the Taliban, which has maintained its close alliance with al-Qaeda, is resurgent and today holds more ground in the country since the U.S. ousted the jihadists in early 2002.

And the threat posed by jihadist groups in Afghanistan has expanded. The Islamic State has established a small, but significant, foothold in the country. Pakistani jihadist groups that are hostile to the U.S. – such as the Movement of the Taliban in Pakistan, Lashkar-e-Taiba, and Harakat-ul-Muhajideen – operate bases inside Afghanistan as well.

U.S. Estimates on al-Qaeda in Afghanistan Were Incorrect

For nearly seven years, the Obama administration wrote off al-Qaeda as a spent force. The group has been described as "decimated."[1] After Osama bin Laden was killed in Pakistan, President Obama said the "core of al-Qaeda in Pakistan and Afghanistan is on a path to defeat."[2] The Obama administration pushed this narrative hard, with many counterterrorism analysts adopting the line that al-Qaeda was either defeated or close to it.[3]

Between 2010 and 2016, Obama administration officials, including CIA Director Leon Panetta, as well as other U.S. military and intelligence officials, characterized al-Qaeda's presence in Afghanistan as minimal and consistently told the American public that the group has a presence of just 50 to 100 fighters. "I think at most, we're looking at maybe 50 to 100, maybe less. It's in that vicinity. There's no question that the main location of al-Qaeda is in tribal areas of Pakistan," Panetta said on ABC News This Week.[4]

This assessment, which contradicted the U.S. military's own press releases announcing raids against al-Qaeda in Afghanistan,[5] was consistently repeated by U.S. intelligence and military officials. In June 2015, the U.S. military claimed in its biannual Enhancing Security and Stability in Afghanistan report that al-Qaeda "has a sustained presence in Afghanistan of probably fewer

---

[1] Joseph Straw, "Most of Al Qaeda's big names have been either captured or killed, but some remain," *NY Daily News*, July 21, 2013. (http://www.nydailynews.com/news/world/al-qaeda-decimated-not-obliterated-article-1.1405185)
[2] Susan Crabtree, "FLASHBACK: Obama: Al Qaeda is on 'a path to defeat'; calls for resetting terror policy," *The Washington Times*, May 23, 2013. (http://www.washingtontimes.com/news/2013/may/23/obama-al-qaeda-is-on-a-path-to-defeat/)
[3] For example: Peter Bergen, "Time to declare victory: al Qaeda is defeated," *CNN's Security Clearance*, June 27, 2012. (http://security.blogs.cnn.com/2012/06/27/time-to-declare-victory-al-qaeda-is-defeated-opinion/)
[4] Felicia Sonmez and Matt DeLong, "Panetta: 50-100 al-Qaeda remain in Afghanistan," *The Washington Post*, June 27, 2010. (http://voices.washingtonpost.com/44/2010/06/panetta-50-100-al-qaeda-remain.html?wprss=44)
[5] Bill Roggio and Patrick Megahan, "ISAF raids against al Qaeda and allies in Afghanistan 2007-2013," *FDD's Long War Journal*, May 30, 2014. (http://www.longwarjournal.org/archives/2014/05/al_qaeda_and_allies.php)

Bill Roggio   April 27, 2017

than 100 operatives concentrated largely in Kunar and Nuristan Provinces, where they remain year-round."[6] The December 2015 report claimed that al-Qaeda is "primarily concentrated in the east and northeast."[7]

This estimate of al-Qaeda's strength, which consistently downplayed al-Qaeda's presence in Afghanistan, came crashing down in mid-October 2015, when the U.S. military and Afghan forces orchestrated a large-scale operation against two al-Qaeda camps in the Shorabak district in the southern Afghan province of Kandahar.[8]

The scale of al-Qaeda's presence at the two camps in Shorabak quickly disproved the longstanding 50 to 100 estimate. A U.S. military statement, quoting spokesman Brigadier General Wilson Shoffner, described the raid as "one of the largest joint ground-assault operations we have ever conducted in Afghanistan."[9] It took U.S. and Afghan forces more than four days to clear the two camps, with the aid of 63 airstrikes.

Shoffner's description of the al-Qaeda facilities indicated that they had been built long ago. "The first site, a well-established training camp, spanned approximately one square mile. The second site covered nearly 30 square miles," Shoffner said. "We struck a major al-Qaeda sanctuary in the center of the Taliban's historic heartland," he added.[10]

Weeks later, General John F. Campbell, then the commander of U.S. Forces - Afghanistan and NATO's Resolute Support mission, described one of the camps, which was run by al-Qaeda in the Indian Subcontinent (AQIS), al-Qaeda's branch in South Asia, as "probably the largest training camp-type facility that we have seen in 14 years of war."[11]

It has been estimated that at least 150 al-Qaeda fighters were killed during the raids on the two camps in Shorabak. This is 50 more al-Qaeda fighters than the upper end of the Obama administration's estimate of al-Qaeda's strength throughout all of Afghanistan. And the al-Qaeda members were killed in southern Afghanistan, not in the northeastern provinces of Kunar and Nuristan, where we have been told they were concentrated.[12]

---

[6] Department of Defense, "Report on Enhancing Security and Stability in Afghanistan," June 2015. (https://news.usni.org/wp-content/uploads/2015/06/June_1225_Report_Final1.pdf)

[7] Department of Defense, "Enhancing Security and Stability in Afghanistan," December 2015. (https://www.defense.gov/Portals/1/Documents/pubs/1225_Report_Dec_2015_-_Final_20151210.pdf)

[8] Thomas Joscelyn and Bill Roggio, "US military strikes large al Qaeda training camps in southern Afghanistan," *FDD's Long War Journal*, October 13, 2015. (http://www.longwarjournal.org/archives/2015/10/us-military-strikes-large-al-qaeda-training-camps-in-southern-afghanistan.php)

[9] Ibid.

[10] Nick Paton Walsh, Jason Hanna, and Mark Morgenstein, "Al Qaeda sites in Afghanistan dismantled in joint operation, U.S. military says," *CNN*, October 13, 2015. (http://www.cnn.com/2015/10/13/asia/afghanistan-al-qaeda-us/index.html)

[11] Dan Lamothe, "'Probably the largest' al-Qaeda training camp ever destroyed in Afghanistan," *The Washington Post*, October 30, 2015. (https://www.washingtonpost.com/news/checkpoint/wp/2015/10/30/probably-the-largest-al-qaeda-training-camp-ever-destroyed-in-afghanistan/?utm_term=.ad1c23c34fd1)

[12] Bill Roggio, "US military insists al Qaeda is 'concentrated' in Afghan east and northeast," *FDD's Long War Journal*, December 16, 2015. (http://www.longwarjournal.org/archives/2015/12/us-military-insists-al-qaeda-is-concentrated-in-afghan-east-and-northeast.php)

Bill Roggio   April 27, 2017

The U.S. military was ultimately forced to concede its estimate of al-Qaeda's strength in Afghanistan was wrong. In mid-December 2016, General Nicholson admitted that the U.S. military killed or captured 50 al-Qaeda leaders and an additional 200 operatives during calendar year 2016 in Afghanistan.[13]

In April 2016, Major General Jeff Buchanan, Resolute Support's deputy chief of staff, told CNN that the 50 to 100 estimate was incorrect based on the results of the Shorabak raid. "If you go back to last year, there were a lot of intel estimates that said within Afghanistan al-Qaeda probably has 50 to 100 members, but in this one camp we found more than 150," he said. The estimate of al-Qaeda operatives in Afghanistan was revised upwards to about 300.[14]

However, well before the Shorabak raids, it was evident to those of us closely watching the war in Afghanistan that al-Qaeda was stronger in Afghanistan than the official estimates, and was not confined to small areas in the northeast. Al-Qaeda consistently reported on its operations throughout Afghanistan, and the U.S. military, up until the summer of 2013, reported on raids against al-Qaeda cells in multiple provinces.

Surely, there was something seriously wrong with the CIA and the U.S. military's ability to properly report on al-Qaeda's presence in Afghanistan.

Al-Qaeda's footprint inside Afghanistan remains a direct threat to U.S. national security and, with the resurgence of the Taliban, it is a threat that is only growing stronger.

The Enduring Taliban-al-Qaeda Relationship

Al-Qaeda's presence in Afghanistan has not occurred in a vacuum. It has maintained its strength in the country since the U.S. invasion, launched a new branch, AQIS, and established training camps with the help and support of the Taliban.

When Generals Campbell and Buchanan discussed al-Qaeda in the wake of the Shorabak raid, they described the group as resurgent. Campbell described the Taliban-al-Qaeda relationship as a "renewed partnership," while Buchanan said it "has since 'grown stronger.'"[15]

But like the estimate that al-Qaeda maintained a small cadre of 50 to 100 operatives in Afghanistan between 2010 and 2016, the idea that the Taliban and al-Qaeda have only recently reinvigorated their relationship is incorrect. Al-Qaeda would not have been able to maintain a large cadre of fighters and leaders inside Afghanistan, conduct operations in 25 of Afghanistan's

---

[13] Thomas Joscelyn and Bill Roggio, "US military: 250 al Qaeda operatives killed or captured in Afghanistan this year," *FDD's Long War Journal*, December 14, 2016. (http://www.longwarjournal.org/archives/2016/12/us-military-250-al-qaeda-operatives-killed-or-captured-in-afghanistan-this-year.php)

[14] Nick Patton Walsh, "Al Qaeda 'very active' in Afghanistan: U.S. Commander," *CNN*, April 13, 2016. (http://www.cnn.com/2016/04/13/middleeast/afghanistan-al-qaeda/)

[15] Thomas Joscelyn and Bill Roggio, "US military admits al Qaeda is stronger in Afghanistan than previously estimated," *FDD's Long War Journal*, April 13, 2016. (http://www.longwarjournal.org/archives/2016/04/us-military-admits-al-qaeda-is-stronger-in-afghanistan-than-previously-estimated.php)

34 provinces, establish training camps, and relocate high-level leaders from Pakistan's tribal areas to Afghanistan without the Taliban's long-term support.

Al-Qaeda has remained loyal to the Taliban's leader, which it describes as the Amir al-Mumineen, or the "Commander of the Faithful," since the U.S. invaded Afghanistan in 2001. Osama bin Laden maintained his oath of allegiance to Mullah Omar, the Taliban's founder and first emir.[16] When bin Laden died, Ayman al-Zawahiri renewed that oath.[17] And when Mullah Omar's death was announced in 2015, Zawahiri swore *bayat* (an oath of allegiance) to Mullah Mansour, the Taliban's new leader.[18] Mansour publicly accepted Zawahiri's oath.[19]

The close relationship between the two jihadist groups is also evident with the assent of the Taliban's new deputy emir, Sirajuddin Haqqani, who leads the powerful Taliban subgroup known as the Haqqani Network. Sirajuddin and the Haqqani Network have maintained close ties to al-Qaeda for years. The relationship is evident in the U.S. government's designations of multiple Haqqani Network leaders. Two documents seized from Osama bin Laden's compound show that Siraj has closely coordinated his operations with al-Qaeda in Afghanistan and Pakistan.[20]

The Taliban-al-Qaeda relationship remains strong to this day. And with the Taliban gaining control of a significant percentage of Afghanistan's territory, al-Qaeda has more areas to plant its flag.[21]

Rise of the Islamic State

Shortly after Abu Bakr al-Baghdadi declared the establishment of the caliphate in 2014, announcing the formation of the Islamic State, a small number of disgruntled jihadists from the

---

[16] Thomas Joscelyn, "Analysis: Al Qaeda attempts to undermine new Islamic State with old video of Osama bin Laden," *FDD's Long War Journal*, July 14, 2014.
(http://www.longwarjournal.org/archives/2014/07/osama_bin_laden_disc.php#)
[17] Thomas Joscelyn, "Al Qaeda renews its oath of allegiance to Taliban leader Mullah Omar," *FDD's Long War Journal*, July 21, 2014. (http://www.longwarjournal.org/archives/2014/07/al_qaeda_renews_its.php)
[18] Thomas Joscelyn, "Ayman al Zawahiri pledges allegiance to the Taliban's new emir," *FDD's Long War Journal*, August 13, 2015. (http://www.longwarjournal.org/archives/2015/08/ayman-al-zawahiri-pledges-allegiance-to-the-talibans-new-emir.php) (A translation of Zawahiri's statement was provided by the SITE Intelligence Group.)
[19] Thomas Joscelyn and Bill Roggio, "New Taliban emir accepts al Qaeda's oath of allegiance," *FDD's Long War Journal*, August 14, 2015. (http://www.longwarjournal.org/archives/2015/08/new-taliban-emir-accepts-al-qaedas-oath-of-allegiance.php)
[20] Thomas Joscelyn and Bill Roggio, "The Taliban's new leadership is allied with al Qaeda," *FDD's Long War Journal*, July 31, 2015. (http://www.longwarjournal.org/archives/2015/07/the-talibans-new-leadership-is-allied-with-al-qaeda.php); Thomas Joscelyn, "Osama bin Laden's Files: The Pakistani government wanted to negotiate," *FDD's Long War Journal*, March 9, 2015. (http://www.longwarjournal.org/archives/2015/03/osama-bin-ladens-files-the-pakistani-government-wanted-to-negotiate.php)
[21] Bill Roggio, "Afghan Taliban lists 'Percent of Country under the control of Mujahideen,'" *FDD's Long War Journal*, March 28, 2017. (http://www.longwarjournal.org/archives/2017/03/afghan-taliban-lists-percent-of-country-under-the-control-of-mujahideen.php)

Bill Roggio   April 27, 2017

Afghan and Pakistani Taliban, as well as al-Qaeda, discarded their oaths to the Taliban, pledged their fealty to Baghdadi, and established the so-called Khorasan province.[22]

While the Islamic State dominates the jihad in Iraq and is a major player in Syria, the group has posed a smaller threat in Afghanistan and Pakistan when compared to the Taliban, al-Qaeda, and their jihadist allies. The U.S. military estimated the group had upwards of 2,000 fighters at the beginning of 2016, but had lost between 25 and 30 percent of its men in the months that followed.[23] While U.S. military estimates of the strength of jihadist groups in Afghanistan must be taken with a grain of salt, this number is likely in the right ballpark.

The Islamic State has a much smaller presence in Afghanistan when compared to the Taliban. While the Taliban controls or contests more than 200 of Afghanistan's 400 districts, the Islamic State only controls terrain in several districts in the eastern province of Nangarhar. The group also reportedly has a presence in the Afghan north.

The Islamic State's Khorasan province has remained entrenched in Nangarhar and has withstood multiple U.S.-backed offensives over the past two years. The U.S. military has had success in killing key leaders, but the group has proven resilient.

Still, the so-called caliphate's Khorasan province has remained on the margins of the Afghan war. It has conducted a limited number of suicide attacks and other operations in the Afghan capital of Kabul and elsewhere,[24] but has not come close to matching the Taliban's operational tempo.

Khorasan province has had a difficult time gaining traction throughout much of Afghanistan and Pakistan, as it is unwilling to cooperate with other, long-entrenched jihadist groups. In fact, the Taliban crushed the Khorasan province's forces in Helmand, Farah, and Zabul after they demanded that the Taliban's fighters swear allegiance to Baghdadi.

Pakistani Jihadist Groups Operating in Afghanistan

In addition to the Taliban, al-Qaeda, and the Islamic State, numerous Pakistan-based jihadist groups are known to operate in Afghanistan. For the most part, these organizations remain in the Taliban and al-Qaeda sphere, and leaders of the groups often backfill leadership positions when al-Qaeda commanders are killed in U.S. airstrikes.

---

[22] Thomas Joscelyn, "Previously obscure al Qaeda leader responds to dissenters," *FDD's Long War Journal*, May 30, 2014. (http://www.longwarjournal.org/archives/2014/05/post_7-3.php); LWJ Staff, "Pakistani Taliban splinter group again pledges allegiance to Islamic State," *FDD's Long War Journal*, January 13, 2015. (http://www.longwarjournal.org/archives/2015/01/video_pakistani_tali_2.php)

[23] Thomas Joscelyn, "American soldier killed fighting Islamic State in Afghanistan," *FDD's Long War Journal*, April 8, 2017. (http://www.longwarjournal.org/archives/2017/04/american-soldier-killed-fighting-islamic-state-in-afghanistan.php)

[24] For example: Bill Roggio, "Islamic State claims suicide attack outside Afghanistan's supreme court," *FDD's Long War Journal*, February 8, 2017. (http://www.longwarjournal.org/archives/2017/02/islamic-state-claims-suicide-attack-outside-afghanistans-supreme-court.php)

Bill Roggio   April 27, 2017

The three largest Pakistani groups operating in Afghanistan are the Movement of the Taliban in Pakistan, Lashkar-e-Taiba, and Harakat-ul-Muhajideen.

The Movement of the Taliban in Pakistan (TTP) is largely made up of Taliban groups from Pakistan's tribal areas. It is closely allied with the Afghan Taliban and al-Qaeda. In 2010, the TTP organized the Times Square bombing plot.[25]

The TTP has taken advantage of the turbulent and ungoverned Afghan-Pakistani border to shift its base of operations when the Pakistani military targets it in offensives. The U.S. has killed several TTP leaders in airstrikes in Afghanistan.

Lashkar-e-Taiba (LeT) is a dangerous jihadist group that is backed by Pakistan's military and Inter-Services Intelligence Directorate. The LeT is known to operate training camps in Afghanistan and attacked the Indian Consulate in Herat in 2014.[26] The U.S. has killed several senior LeT operatives in airstrikes in northeastern Afghanistan over the years. The U.S. has also listed several senior LeT operatives, including Hafiz Saeed, the group's emir, as Specially Designated Global Terrorists.

Harakat-ul-Mujahideen (HuM) is another Pakistani jihadist group that is known, as of August 2014, to operate training camps in Afghanistan.[27] HuM has been involved in numerous acts of terror in the region, including hijacking an Indian airplane, attacking the U.S. Consulate in Karachi, and murdering *Wall Street Journal* reporter Daniel Pearl.[28]

---

[25] Anne E. Kornblut and Karin Brulliard, "U.S. blames Pakistani Taliban for Times Square bomb plot," *The Washington Post*, May 10, 2010. (http://www.washingtonpost.com/wp-dyn/content/article/2010/05/09/AR2010050901143.html)

[26] Bill Roggio, "LeT designation notes group's recent attack in western Afghanistan," *FDD's Long War Journal*, June 25, 2014. (http://www.longwarjournal.org/archives/2014/06/let_designation_notes_groups_r.php)

[27] Bill Roggio, "Harakat-ul-Mujahideen 'operates terrorist training camps in eastern Afghanistan,'" *FDD's Long War Journal*, August 8, 2014. (http://www.longwarjournal.org/archives/2014/08/harakat-ul-mujahidee.php)

[28] Thomas Joscelyn, "New investigation into murder of Daniel Pearl released," *FDD's Long War Journal*, January 21, 2011. (http://www.longwarjournal.org/archives/2011/01/new_investigation_in.php)

14

Mr. POE. The Chair recognizes Dr. Jones for 5 minutes.

STATEMENT OF SETH G. JONES, PH.D., DIRECTOR, INTER-NATIONAL SECURITY AND DEFENSE POLICY CENTER, RAND CORPORATION

Mr. JONES. Thank you, Chairman Poe, Ranking Member Keating, and other distinguished members of the subcommittee. Thanks for holding this hearing. It is a reminder that Afghanistan is and should be still important.

At over a decade and a half after the 9/11 attacks, many Americans may not realize how deeply engaged the U.S. remains in Afghanistan. Most of the media coverage, up until very recently, has been on counterterrorism operations in Syria, Iraq, North Korea, and a range of other locations, but Afghanistan is a front line state. Many may also forget that the number of U.S. military forces there, which is in the neighborhood of 8,400, is larger than any other active combat zone deployment. It is larger than what the U.S. has in Syria, Iraq, or other combat zones. As Bill mentioned earlier, some Americans finally began to realize and remember that we still have forces there after the U.S. dropped its most powerful, or one of its most powerful non-nuclear bombs.

My comments are going to focus on three questions. First, what are U.S. national security interests in Afghanistan today? That is one. Two, what is the terrorist and insurgent landscape? And then three, what, at least briefly, steps can the U.S. do to help mitigate the threat from Afghanistan and more broadly in the region?

So, let me turn to U.S. interests. I mean, I think there is no question that the U.S. has a range of interests overseas. I mentioned earlier Russia, China, North Korea, and Iran, but I do think the U.S. has several interests that remain in Afghanistan. One is that there are a number of extremist groups, Islamic extremist groups, that continue to operate on both sides of the Afghan-Pakistan border. Bill mentioned them earlier. They range from al-Qaeda, the Taliban, Haqqani Network to the Islamic State, but also a range of other ones that have operations in Central Asia.

Second, I think an expanding war, if the U.S. were to leave, would also increase regional instability particularly with countries like India, Pakistan, Iran, Russia, and even China. A particular concern to me would be what it does to the Pakistan-India competition. Those are both nuclear armed states and have gone to war and are essentially fighting a proxy war in Afghanistan right now. Let me then move to the landscape, because I think this is important to remember. It is part of U.S. interests. The Taliban does continue to operate. It is the largest group that operates in Afghanistan. It does have its sanctuary, its command and control nodes, in Pakistan not in Afghanistan. Its three major regional surahs are also on the Pakistan side of the border. And I would just emphasize again the chairman's remarks about the increase in Russian contacts and, at least, limited support to the Taliban. It is not a positive step in developments in the region.

But I would point out with the Taliban, the Taliban does not control yet—I mean I would certainly argue that it has increased its rural presence. It does not control yet a major urban area, which makes it a little different from what we have seen in 2014, 2015 in Iraq in cities like Mosul or other cities within Anbar.

AQIS, al-Qaeda in the Indian Subcontinent, my estimate is probably larger and more expansive than it was 5 to 10 years ago. It has a presence that is larger than just what some Americans have talked about up in the northeast; but down in the south in Kandahar as Bill mentioned, in Helmand, along the Baramcha area, in Zabul, in Ghazni, in Paktika, those are likely small cell structures.

In addition, the Islamic State-Khorasan Province does have a presence. It looks to me like it has probably come down a little bit from a year or 2 ago—down to between 1,000 and 2,000 fighters—but I would say that it has conducted a number of attacks both in Afghanistan and Pakistan as well as in Bangladesh. So, in my view it has been pretty active in conducting attacks. There are other groups, the Tehrik-i-Taliban Pakistan, Lashkar-e-Taiba, and Jamaat-ul-Ahrar that also have a presence in the region, and I think—in that sense—there are a milieu of groups.

Just briefly, I would note there are a range of things. I would support the ranking member's comments about focusing on governance and development. I would add electoral reform. I would also add, I think there are opportunities at the moment for reconciliation. I certainly would support at least opening up discussions. I think they are probably unlikely in the near term, but I think they are worth talking about.

The range of things, and we can certainly get into this that—I would suggest pushing U.S. trainers down to the tactical level. I would support probably slightly increasing the U.S. presence in Afghanistan but more on the trade, advise, and assist efforts. And I am happy to talk more later about the steps toward Pakistan, but let me just briefly conclude by noting that the Afghan Government and generally these people want the U.S. to stay, so I think we should take that seriously. Thank you.

[The prepared statement of Mr. Jones follows:]

Managing the Long War

U.S. Policy toward Afghanistan and the Region

Seth G. Jones

CT-472

Testimony presented before the House Foreign Affairs Committee, Subcommittee on Terrorism, Nonproliferation, and Trade on April 27, 2017.

17

For more information on this publication, visit www.rand.org/pubs/testimonies/CT472.html

Testimonies

RAND testimonies record testimony presented or submitted by RAND associates to federal, state, or local legislative committees; government-appointed commissions and panels; and private review and oversight bodies.

www.rand.org

Managing the Long War:
U.S. Policy toward Afghanistan and the Region[1]

Testimony of Seth G. Jones[2]
The RAND Corporation[3]

Before the Committee on Foreign Affairs
Subcommittee on Terrorism, Nonproliferation, and Trade
United States House of Representatives

April 27, 2017

Over a decade and a half after the 9/11 attacks, the United States remains deeply engaged in Afghanistan. While most media coverage of U.S. counterterrorism operations overseas has focused on Syria and Iraq, Afghanistan is still an important frontline state in the struggle against terrorist groups. There are more U.S. military forces (approximately 8,400 soldiers) deployed to Afghanistan than any other active combat zone, and a range of Islamic extremist groups—from the Taliban to al-Qaeda and Islamic State—have a sanctuary in Afghanistan and the region. In April 2017, the United States dropped one of its most powerful non-nuclear bombs—a GBU-43/B massive ordnance air blast bomb—against an Islamic State network of fortified underground tunnels in the eastern province of Nangarhar, temporarily bringing U.S. operations in Afghanistan back to the public's attention. Still, the U.S. presence in Afghanistan remains controversial. Some argue that the United States has little or no strategic

---

[1] This testimony relies in part on such recently published work by the author as Seth G. Jones, James Dobbins, Daniel Byman, Christopher S. Chivvis, Ben Connable, Jeffrey Martini, Eric Robinson, and Nathan Chandler, *Rolling Back the Islamic State*, Santa Monica, Calif.: RAND Corporation, RR-1912, 2017; "How Trump Should Manage Afghanistan: A Realistic Set of Goals for the New Administration," *Foreign Affairs*, March 21, 2017; "Afghanistan," in Xenia Wickett, ed., *America's International Role Under Donald Trump*, London: Chatham House, January 2017; and *Strategic Reversal in Afghanistan*, Contingency Planning Memorandum No. 29, New York: Council on Foreign Relations, June 2016.

[2] The opinions and conclusions expressed in this testimony are the author's alone and should not be interpreted as representing those of the RAND Corporation or any of the sponsors of its research.

[3] The RAND Corporation is a research organization that develops solutions to public policy challenges to help make communities throughout the world safer and more secure, healthier and more prosperous. RAND is nonprofit, nonpartisan, and committed to the public interest.

interests in Afghanistan.[4] As one *Chicago Tribune* reporter concluded, "we have no prospect for victory [in Afghanistan] and no appetite for what it would take even to gain the upper hand. In truth, we have already lost that war."[5] Others have contended that the United States wasted substantial sums of money on reconstruction and development projects.[6]

In light of these views, this testimony focuses on U.S. counterterrorism operations in Afghanistan and asks the following questions. What are U.S. national security interests in Afghanistan today? What is the terrorist and insurgent landscape in Afghanistan and the region?[7] What can the United States do to mitigate the threat from Afghanistan and South Asia?

U.S. Interests in Afghanistan

The United States has a range of national security interests overseas, such as balancing against major powers like Russia and China, containing North Korea, preventing Iran from acquiring nuclear weapons, and targeting Islamic State and other extremist groups in countries like Iraq and Syria. But the United States also has important national security interests in Afghanistan.

First, several extremist groups, such as al-Qaeda, the Taliban, and Islamic State, have a presence in Afghanistan. Additional Taliban advances on the battlefield or a U.S. withdrawal would likely allow al-Qaeda, Islamic State, and other groups—such as Tehreek-e-Taliban Pakistan, Lashkar-e-Taiba, and Jamaat-ul-Ahrar—to increase their presence in Afghanistan. Second, an expanding war could increase regional instability if India, Pakistan, Iran, and Russia were to support a mix of Afghan central government forces, militias, and insurgent groups. Washington has a specific interest in preventing a major escalation in great power conflict in the region, particularly between nuclear-armed Pakistan and India. These states remain engaged in a proxy war in Afghanistan, with New Delhi aiding the Afghan government and Islamabad abetting some insurgent groups, like the Taliban.[8] Third, a U.S. military departure from Afghanistan could foster a perception, however misplaced, that the United States is not a reliable ally. At this point, extremist groups would likely view a withdrawal of U.S. military forces as

---

[4] See Jeffrey Sachs, "U.S. Military Should Get Out of the Middle East," *Boston Globe*, April 3, 2017; A. Trevor Thrall, "Why It's So Hard to Leave Afghanistan," *National Interest*, January 28, 2016; Richard N. Haass, "The Irony of American Strategy," *Foreign Affairs*, Vol. 92, No. 3, May–June 2013, pp. 57–67.

[5] Steve Chapman, "Trump Should End the U.S. War in Afghanistan," *Chicago Tribune*, March 2, 2017.

[6] See reports from the Special Inspector General for Afghanistan Reconstruction (SIGAR). Available at https://www.sigar.mil/allreports/index.aspx?SSR=5.

[7] This testimony uses the terms *insurgency* and *terrorism*. *Insurgency* is a political and military campaign by a nonstate group or groups to overthrow a regime or secede from a country. Insurgent groups are nonstate organizations that use violence—and the threat of violence—to control territory. Insurgency can be understood, in part, as a process of alternative state-building. Groups often tax populations in areas they control, establish justice systems, and attempt to provide other services. *Terrorism*, on the other hand, is a tactic that involves the use of politically motivated violence against noncombatants to cause intimidation or fear among a target audience. Most insurgent groups employ terrorism, but many terrorist groups are not insurgents because they do not control—or aspire to control—territory.

[8] See Khalid Homayun Nadiri, "Old Habits, New Consequences: Pakistan's Posture Toward Afghanistan Since 2001," *International Security*, Fall 2014, Vol. 39, No. 2, pp. 132–168.

their most important victory since the departure of Soviet forces from Afghanistan in 1989. In addition, most European allies have indicated that they would likely withdraw their military forces in the event of an American exit, leaving behind regional powers with conflicting interests.

Given substantial Afghan government weaknesses and the country's nearly perpetual state of war since the 1970s, it is important for the United States to set realistic goals in Afghanistan. The United States should establish an enduring partnership with Afghanistan and leave a small but durable military and diplomatic presence. But it should set limited objectives: prevent the Taliban from overthrowing the Afghan government, pursue political reconciliation with those parts of the Taliban willing to negotiate, and target terrorist and insurgent groups that threaten the United States. Left to the Taliban, Afghanistan would continue to be a crossroads for various Islamic extremist groups. Combating terrorist groups in Afghanistan must therefore be part of a broader campaign to support an Afghan government willing to cooperate in the suppression of such groups.

The Terrorist and Insurgent Landscape

A range of terrorist and insurgent groups are present in Afghanistan and the region. This section examines the most important groups: the Afghan Taliban; al-Qaeda in the Indian Subcontinent; Islamic State–Khorasan Province; and other groups like Lashkar-e-Taiba, Tehreek-e-Taliban Pakistan, and Jamaat-ul-Ahrar.

Afghan Taliban

The Taliban is the largest of these groups and continues to wage an insurgency against the Afghan government. Since the drawdown in the U.S. and NATO troop presence, the Taliban has slowly increased its control of rural territory in Afghanistan, particularly in such provinces as Uruzgan and Helmand.[9] It also continues to conduct complex attacks in major cities like Kabul. The Haqqani network, whose leaders sit on the Taliban's senior shura, has perpetrated some of the most spectacular terrorist attacks in Afghanistan. The Taliban and Haqqani network have benefited from a sanctuary in Pakistan, where their leadership resides and where they receive some aid from the Pakistani government, as well as limited support from neighboring states like Russia and Iran. Russia has increased its contacts with the Taliban and provided limited support out of concern that U.S. military forces may withdraw from the region; as part of a broader strategy to increase Russian influence across the globe; and to weaken Islamic State.[10] Still, the Taliban does not control any major cities and has failed to establish a strong popular support base in Afghanistan.

---

[9] See U.S. military data in Special Inspector General for Afghanistan Reconstruction, *Quarterly Report to the United States Congress,* Arlington, Va., January 30, 2017, pp. 89–91.

[10] See, for example, the comments from Secretary of Defense James Mattis in Tom Bowman, "Defense Secretary Expresses Concern Over Russian Support For Taliban," *National Public Radio*, March 31, 2017.

Al-Qaeda in the Indian Subcontinent

Al-Qaeda has a long history of activity in the region, dating back to the group's formation by Osama bin Laden in the late 1980s. Core al-Qaeda, which includes the group's global leadership, has been severely reduced in size and capability because of persistent U.S. strikes. Ayman al-Zawahiri remains al-Qaeda's leader and is flanked by such individuals as general manager Abd al-Rahman al-Maghrebi and senior manager Abu Muhammad al-Masri. In addition, a small number of al-Qaeda leaders are likely in nearby Iran with ties to the leadership, including Saif al-Adel and Abu Muhammad al-Masri.[11]

In September 2014, Zawahiri announced the creation of al-Qaeda in the Indian Subcontinent (AQIS) as a regional affiliate dedicated to establishing an extreme emirate in South Asia.[12] As Zawahiri argued, "A new branch of al-Qaeda was established and is Qaedat al-Jihad in the Indian Subcontinent, seeking to raise the flag of jihad, return the Islamic rule, and empowering the shariah of Allah across the Indian subcontinent."[13] The group is led by Asim Umar, an Indian, who was a former member of Harkat-ul-Jihad al-Islami, a Pakistan-based terrorist group with branches across the Indian subcontinent.[14] Umar is flanked by Abu Zar, his first deputy. In October 2015, U.S. and Afghan forces targeted a large training camp in Kandahar Province, killing over one hundred operatives linked to AQIS.[15]

AQIS's presence in Afghanistan and the region poses a threat to the United States, though the group has struggled to conduct attacks. The group boasts several hundred members and has cells in such southern and eastern Afghanistan provinces as Helmand, Kandahar, Zabul, Paktika, Ghazni, and Nuristan. AQIS's current size and presence today is almost certainly larger and more expansive than what al-Qaeda had in Afghanistan five or even ten years ago.[16] This expansion may be due in part to Taliban advances in Afghanistan and AQIS's relationship with operatives from the Taliban and other groups, such as Tehreek-e-Taliban Pakistan and Lashkar-e-Jhangvi. AQIS's operatives in Bangladesh have been particularly active, conducting a range of attacks over the past year. In addition, AQIS conducts a steady propaganda campaign from its media arm, Al-Sahab.

Still, AQIS has not conducted many attacks in Afghanistan or Pakistan. It was involved in a high-profile plot in the port of Karachi in 2014, which was foiled by Pakistan security agencies. AQIS operatives have also plotted attacks against U.S. targets in Pakistan, including the U.S. embassy in Islamabad. The United States, Afghanistan, and Pakistan have also killed or captured

---

[11] On the history of al-Qaeda in Iran, see Seth G. Jones, "Al Qaeda in Iran: Why Tehran Is Accommodating the Terrorist Group," *Foreign Affairs*, January 29, 2012.

[12] Ayman al-Zawahiri, audio message, September 2014.

[13] Bill Rogio, "Al Qaeda Opens Branch in the 'Indian Subcontinent,'" *Long War Journal*, September 3, 2014.

[14] Thomas Joscelyn, "Al Qaeda in the Indian Subcontinent Claims Killing of LGBT Activist, Friend in Bangladesh," *Long War Journal*, April 26, 2016.

[15] Dan Lamothe, "'Probably the Largest' Al-Qaeda Training Camp Ever Destroyed in Afghanistan," *Washington Post*, October 30, 2015.

[16] See Richard Esposito, Matthew Cole, and Brian Ross, "President Obama's Secret: Only 100 al Qaeda Now in Afghanistan," *ABC News*, December 2, 2009.

several AQIS operatives, including Ahmed Farouq in January 2015, Qari Imran in January 2015, and Farouq al-Qatari in October 2016.

Islamic State–Khorasan Province

Since 2014, Islamic State has attempted to expand a beachhead in South Asia by leveraging existing militant networks. Islamic State leaders have called this land "Wilayat Khorasan," a reference to the historical region that encompassed parts of Iran, Central Asia, Afghanistan, and Pakistan.[17] Yet Islamic State–Khorasan Province, as Islamic State leaders refer to this branch, controls virtually no territory except for tiny areas in Deh Bala, Achin, and Naziyan Districts in Nangarhar Province of eastern Afghanistan. Islamic State–Khorasan Province has conducted a handful of attacks, but has failed to secure the support of most locals, struggled with poor leadership, and faced determined opposition from other local insurgent groups, most notably the Taliban.

By co-opting local networks, such as disaffected members of Tehreek-e-Taliban Pakistan and the Afghan Taliban, Islamic State–Khorasan Province has established an organizational structure led by an emir, a deputy emir, and a central shura with such committees as intelligence, finance, propaganda, and education. After the death of leader Hafiz Saeed Khan in 2016 from a U.S. strike, Islamic State appointed Abdul Hasib, a former Afghan Taliban member, as emir of Islamic State–Khorasan Province. Islamic State leaders reached out to other militant groups in the region. Today, Islamic State–Khorasan Province includes roughly 1,000 to 2,000 fighters, a slight decrease from 2015.[18] The group has also conducted a small number of attacks in the region, such as against a military hospital in Kabul in March 2017, a police convoy in Quetta in August 2016, Pakistani attorneys at a hospital in Quetta in August 2016, Hazara protesters in Kabul in July 2016, and the Pakistani consulate in Jalalabad in January 2016.[19]

As Figure 1 shows, Islamic State territorial control in Afghanistan peaked in spring 2015, when it controlled an estimated 511,777 people (1.9 percent of Afghanistan's population) and roughly 2,919 square kilometers (less than 1 percent of Afghanistan's territory). Most of this territory was in the southwestern province of Farah and eastern province of Nangarhar, with small pockets in other provinces, such as Helmand. By winter 2016–2017, Islamic State control

---

[17] *Khorasan* comes from the Persian language and means "where the sun arrives from."

[18] Author interviews with U.S., Pakistani, and Afghan officials in 2016 and 2017. Several reports have almost certainly vastly overstated the size of Islamic State—Khorasan Province, putting it between 9,000 and 11,000. See, for example, Antonio Giustozzi, "The Islamic State in 'Khorasan': A Nuanced View," London: Royal United Services Institute, February 5, 2016.

[19] Mujib Mashal and Fahim Abedmarch, "After Deadly Attack on Kabul Hospital, 'Everywhere Was Full of Blood,'" *New York Times*, March 8, 2017; Shafqat Ali, "70 Dead as Taliban Bomb Protest over Lawyer's Killing in Quetta," *Nation* (Pakistan), August 8, 2016; Kunwar Khuldune Shahid, "What Quetta Bombing Reveals About Islamic State and Pakistani Taliban," *Diplomat*, August 9, 2016; Syed Ali Shah, "14 Injured as Roadside Bomb Targets Judge's Police Escort in Quetta," *Dawn* (Pakistan), August 11, 2016; "Afghanistan Mourns Protest Blast Victims." *Al Jazeera*, July 23, 2016; Khalid Alokozay and Mujib Mashal, "ISIS Claims Assault that Killed 7 Near Pakistani Consulate in Afghanistan," *New York Times*, January 13, 2016.

23

had decreased to only 64,406 people (an 87-percent drop) and 372 square kilometers (also an 87-percent drop) from 2015 levels.[20]

Figure 1: Islamic State Control of Territory in Afghanistan[21]

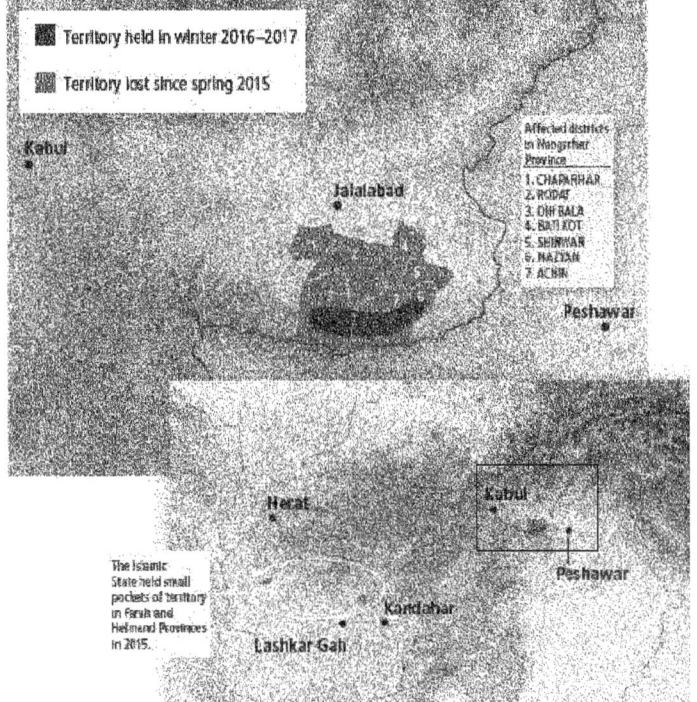

Other Groups

In addition, fighters from other militant groups, such as Tehreek-e-Taliban Pakistan, Lashkar-e-Taiba, and Jamaat-ul-Ahrar, are also involved in the insurgency in Afghanistan. The Obama administration focused on counterterrorism operations against al-Qaeda rather than counterinsurgency operations against the Taliban, yet counterterrorism and counterinsurgency are deeply interlinked in Afghanistan. Territory controlled by the Taliban has been used—and will likely continue to be used—by terrorist groups to plan for and conduct attacks in Afghanistan, the region, and perhaps globally.

[20] Jones et al., 2017.

[21] Jones et al., 2017.

Policy Considerations

U.S. objectives in Afghanistan should be realistic and limited. Accomplishing U.S. objectives will require a steadfast commitment from the United States and its partners to strengthen national and local governance; establish a more enduring security commitment; revise U.S. policy toward the region, including changing Pakistan's strategic calculus; and continuing to provide economic and humanitarian support.

Strengthen National and Local Governance

Improving governance is important for the ultimate success of counterterrorism and counterinsurgency operations in Afghanistan and the region. Militant groups can take advantage of weak governance. Afghanistan ranks among the worst countries in the world in every category of governance—accountability, political stability, government effectiveness, regulatory quality, rule of law, and control of corruption—according to World Bank estimates.[22] Pakistan is not far behind, ranking among the bottom 30 percent of countries worldwide in each of these categories.[23]

Better national and local governance is particularly important in Afghanistan, where the country faces a burgeoning insurgency that has allowed militant groups to gain a foothold.[24] Significant problems continue to plague Afghanistan's National Unity Government, such as widespread corruption, deteriorating economic conditions, disagreements over reconciliation with the Taliban, and competition for power among political elites. President Ashraf Ghani has clashed with the Afghan Parliament, and several major political issues remain unresolved. The political agreement that created the National Unity Government, which the United States helped broker, required the Afghan government to hold parliamentary and district council elections. Yet the elections are long overdue. The agreement also stipulated that Afghanistan convene a grand assembly of elders, a *loya jirga*, from across the country to amend the Afghan Constitution and formally establish the position of prime minister. But Afghan political elites disagree about the timing of the elections and electoral reform. Some elites argue that the current election commission lacks legitimacy because of its flawed handling of the 2014 elections. They contend that elections cannot be held until the election process and the Independent Election Commission are reformed.[25]

Washington's most important political priority in Afghanistan should be to focus U.S. efforts on working with the Afghan government and political elites to improve governance and reach a

---

[22] The Worldwide Governance Indicators database, World Bank, 2017. The data are available at www.govindicators.org and were accessed on April 18, 2017.

[23] The Worldwide Governance Indicators data for Pakistan are from 2015. Pakistan is ranked in the bottom 27 percent for voice and accountability, the bottom 1 percent for political stability, the bottom 27 percent for government effectiveness, the bottom 29 percent for regulatory quality, the bottom 24 percent for rule of law, and the bottom 24 percent for control of corruption.

[24] Scott Smith and Colin Cookman, eds., *State Strengthening in Afghanistan: Lessons Learned, 2001–2014*, Washington, D.C.: U.S. Institute of Peace, May 2016.

[25] See Ali Yawar Adili and Martine van Bijlert, "Pushing the Parliament to Accept a Decree: Another Election Without Reform," Kabul: Afghanistan Analysts Network, June 10, 2016.

consensus on contentious issues, such as electoral reform. U.S. diplomats and White House officials were instrumental in negotiating the agreement that led to the National Unity Government and should make a similar effort to overcome the differences on electoral reform to permit legislative elections to go forward. Afghanistan should not hold a *loya jirga* until there is a broader consensus on its ultimate purpose. Poorly organized elections marred by corruption and a contentious *loya jirga* would be more destabilizing than helpful. The United States should also continue to support governance from the bottom up, since tribes, subtribes, clans, and local communities play an influential role in a country with a weak and sometimes unpopular central government.

Without expecting early results, Washington should also continue to encourage and promote regional support for an Afghan-led process of reconciliation with the Taliban. The Obama administration's exit deadlines to withdraw U.S. forces from Afghanistan likely undermined the prospects for peace. While Taliban officials were intermittently willing to engage in peace talks, they were faced with a classic question of "time horizons": Why reach a peace settlement today if their battlefield prospects and bargaining position were likely to improve once U.S. forces and other NATO forces withdrew? Today, the possibility of a small but durable U.S. military and diplomatic presence in Afghanistan may increase the possibility of a settlement, however difficult talks will be.

Establish a More Enduring Security Commitment

The U.S.'s immediate security focus should be building the capacity of Afghan forces to protect populated areas and target terrorist leaders and their support networks. The United States needs to continue partnering with Afghan special operations units (the Ktah Khas, commandos, and Afghan national army special forces), as well as the Afghan National Army, Afghan National Police, and local forces. Over the past several decades, no Afghan government has been able to sustain itself without support from outside powers. This has been particularly true when the country faced a serious security threat, as it does now. It is much cheaper for the United States and its allies to support Afghan security forces than it is to deploy large numbers of U.S. and other North Atlantic Treaty Organization (NATO) soldiers. The United States should carry through on its commitment to providing roughly $4 billion per year through at least 2020 to help sustain the costs of the Ministries of Defense and Interior and improve the retention of quality police and soldiers. The United States should also continue to build up the Afghan Air Force, which is plagued by low operational readiness, maintenance problems, and a lack of trained aircrew.

An aggressive campaign should involve continuing to designate Afghanistan as an area of active hostility for the use of lethal force, giving the U.S. military flexibility to target terrorists.[26] In addition to targeted strikes, U.S. and Afghan government forces need to work closely with tribes, subtribes, clans, and other local actors. In southern parts of Nangarhar, for example, the

---

[26] White House, "Procedures for Approving Direct Action Against Terrorist Targets Located Outside the United States and Areas of Active Hostilities," May 22, 2013. The redacted and declassified document is available at https://fas.org/irp/offdocs/ppd/ppg-procedures.pdf.

population is mostly Ghilzai Pashtun from such tribes as the Shinwaris.[27] Support from these communities, along with such forces as the Afghan Local Police and programs like Village Stability Operations, is important to hold any areas that are cleared.[28]

The new U.S. administration should retain and perhaps modestly increase the current American force of 8,400 soldiers. Afghanistan could be regarded as an important regional base in a global campaign against Islamic extremists and other threats to U.S. interests. Unlike many other Islamic countries, Afghan leaders and most of the population want U.S. forces to stay. The United States should also work closely with countries participating in the NATO-led Resolute Support Mission to sustain their current numbers and roles. As part of a total non-U.S. NATO commitment of around 5,000, these countries include Italy in the west; Germany in the north; and Turkey in the capital region. A sustained U.S.- and NATO-led security role is important, since a larger military role for Afghanistan's neighbors would be either infeasible (Afghans, for instance, continue to harbor animosity toward the Russians for their invasion in the 1980s and are even more hostile to Pakistan), increase regional security competition (a larger Indian security role would likely increase friction with Pakistan), or undermine American interests (an Iranian security role would be unwelcome in Washington).

Revise U.S. Policy toward Pakistan and the Region

There are substantial challenges to regional cooperation. First, there is security competition among major powers, most notably between Pakistan and India. Afghanistan has long been entangled in a "great game" among neighboring states and global powers.[29] Most of Afghanistan's neighbors prefer a stable central government in Kabul but want one that protects their own interests. New Delhi, for example, has enjoyed close relations with the Afghan government and sought to minimize Islamabad's influence and weaken anti-Indian terrorist groups. Pakistan, on the other hand, has attempted to minimize New Delhi's influence in Afghanistan and has supported proxy groups. An enduring U.S. commitment to Afghanistan may help alleviate some, although not all, of this security competition. The rise of Islamic State–Khorasan Province has raised concerns that some countries—such as Iran and Russia—might increase their cooperation with the Taliban to hedge against Islamic State. The Taliban has been effective against Islamic State in such Afghan provinces as Helmand and Farah. But Russian or Iranian cooperation with the Taliban would undermine long-term stability and ensure that the region continues to attract and give rise to violent extremist groups. The United States should

---

[27] See Robert Kemp, "Counterinsurgency in Nangarhar Province, Eastern Afghanistan, 2004–2008," *Military Review*, November–December 2010.

[28] See Ty Connett and Bob Cassidy, "Village Stability Operations: More than Village Defense," *Special Warfare*, Vol. 24, No. 3, July–September 2011.

[29] William Dalrymple, *Return of a King: The Battle for Afghanistan, 1839–42*, New York: Alfred A. Knopf, 2013; Diana Preston, *The Dark Defile: Britain's Catastrophic Invasion of Afghanistan 1838–1842*, New York: Walker & Company, 2012; Steve Coll, *Ghost Wars: The Secret History of the CIA, Afghanistan, and Bin Laden, from the Soviet Invasion to September 10, 2001*, New York: Penguin Press, 2004; Barnett R. Rubin, *The Fragmentation of Afghanistan: State Formation and Collapse in the International System*, New Haven, Conn.: Yale University Press, 1995.

communicate publicly and privately to these countries—particularly Moscow—that the United States will not tolerate support to the Taliban.

Al-Qaeda, Islamic State, and other groups have used Pakistan territory to recruit fighters, secure funding, and conduct operations. The biggest challenge may be curbing Pakistan's support to militant groups, including the Afghan Taliban, which Islamabad uses as a foreign policy tool. While Pakistan security agencies have targeted Islamic State and al-Qaeda operatives, Islamabad's support to other militant groups undermines regional stability. The Afghan Taliban has safe havens within parts of Pakistan and access to funds and equipment. Washington's goal should be to change Pakistan's calculus over time, while recognizing that, whatever policies Washington adopts, Islamabad will likely not alter its Afghanistan policy quickly—even if civilian leaders in Pakistan favor such an outcome.

The United States should review its options for dealing with Pakistan. For example, the United States could take further steps to pressure Taliban sanctuaries within Pakistan, with or without the support of Islamabad. The May 2016 U.S. killing of Mullah Mansour, the head of the Afghan Taliban, while he was traveling in Pakistan indicates the kind of direct action against the Taliban and the Haqqani network that could make an important difference. Congress has reduced military assistance to Pakistan in recent years and curtailed Pakistan's access to foreign military financing. But even today's reduced amounts of U.S. assistance could be cut further. Targeted economic sanctions could be selectively applied against specific organizations and individuals; Washington could encourage other countries to consider similar steps. On the more positive side, Washington might also sketch out a vision of an improved relationship with Pakistan if Islamabad were to cut its ties with militant groups attacking both Afghanistan and India. This outcome would be highly desirable for broader American interests, given Pakistan's central role in the stability of the entire region—and its ability to upend that stability.

In addition, an enduring U.S. commitment to Afghanistan would send a strong signal to Islamabad that the country does not need to prepare for a post-American region, a rationale that Pakistan policymakers repeatedly used to justify their support to the Taliban and other militant groups. With a long-term U.S. commitment to the region, Washington and Islamabad can focus on building a more constructive and enduring political, economic, and security relationship. A U.S. commitment should help allay Pakistan's fears that the country will face an Afghanistan again in chaos or an Afghanistan dominated by India. U.S. goals should be to change Pakistan's calculus over time, while recognizing that whatever policies Washington adopts, Islamabad is not likely to change its Afghanistan policy quickly.

Provide Economic and Humanitarian Support

Economic and humanitarian challenges are acute in Afghanistan because of the government's fragility and the Taliban-led insurgency that has engulfed much of the country. The United States should continue working closely with the United Nations, the World Bank, International Monetary Fund, and major financial contributors to better address serious economic and governance challenges. Rather than focusing on a broad array of economic issues, U.S. diplomats might concentrate on working with organizations like the World Bank and International Monetary Fund to prevent developments that could increase large-scale opposition to the government, such as a poor agricultural harvest, rising unemployment, and a prolonged energy shortage. An electricity blackout, such as the one that occurred in Kabul in January 2016 following the Taliban sabotage of Kabul's main power supply, could decrease morale and increase antigovernment sentiment, particularly if prolonged. Next to Syria, Afghanistan has produced the second-largest number of refugees in the world, at 2.7 million.[30] This number could further increase if American and international support are not sustained.

America Is Still Welcome

Of all the countries in which the United States is engaged against Islamic extremists, Afghanistan is one of the few places where the local government—led by President Ashraf Ghani and chief executive officer Abdullah Abdullah—and the bulk of the local population have welcomed U.S. military forces. Despite this support, there are some powerful figures that object to the U.S. military presence. Among the most vocal is former Afghan president Hamid Karzai, who remarked in April 2017 that he was committed to "ousting the U.S." from Afghanistan.[31] But Karzai does not speak for most Afghans.

U.S. interests in Afghanistan do not diminish the importance of Iraq, Syria, Libya, and other frontline states battling terrorist groups. But the United States should make Afghanistan and neighboring Pakistan an important and enduring part of the struggle against al-Qaeda, Islamic State, and other extremists. Since terrorist groups continue to operate in Afghanistan and the region, the United States must aim the Taliban from overthrowing the Afghan government, pursue political reconciliation where feasible, and target terrorist and insurgent groups that threaten the United States. This approach may not quickly end the war, but it would be an important contribution to U.S., regional, and international security.

---

[30] Data are from the United Nations High Commissioner for Refugees, "Facts and Figures about Refugees," Geneva, 2016.

[31] Mujib Mashal, "Calling Successor a 'Traitor,' Afghan Ex-Leader Denounces U.S. Bombing," *New York Times*, April 15, 2017.

Mr. POE. I thank the gentleman.
Dr. Felbab-Brown, 5 minutes.

STATEMENT OF VANDA FELBAB-BROWN, PH.D., SENIOR FELLOW, CENTER FOR 21ST CENTURY SECURITY AND INTELLIGENCE, FOREIGN POLICY PROGRAM, THE BROOKINGS INSTITUTION

Ms. FELBAB-BROWN. Thank you very much, Chairman Poe, Ranking Member Keating, and distinguished members of the subcommittee. It is an honor for me to address you today.

I want to give away my punch line right at the beginning. Improving governance, not merely beefing up military efforts or attempting to counter external sponsor of terrorism in Afghanistan, is critical for the success of U.S. counterterrorism efforts. It is also critical for the broader interests the United States has in Afghanistan and the region. Yes, denying safe havens to anti-American global and regional terrorist groups is crucial, and it is the number one primary objective.

But, U.S. interests in Afghanistan go beyond that. As Seth also mentioned, an unstable Afghanistan risks destabilizing Pakistan. The relationship is not merely the reverse that a problematic Pakistan destabilizes Afghanistan, but also that an unstable Afghanistan destabilizes Pakistan and, as result, Pakistan-India relationship and the entire region of Central and South Asia.

Moreover, this integration of the Afghan State or an outbreak of an outright civil war would be a great boost to Salafi groups around the world. Once again, a great power will have been seen as being defeated in Afghanistan. That is from a strategic perspective, few places from a counterterrorism point of view matter as much as Afghanistan does. Moreover, U.S. reputation and self-regard are also at stake as a country that can be relied upon to honor its commitments, including commitments to the Afghan people.

The Taliban remains by far the most potent terrorist group in Afghanistan. It has not targeted U.S. assets or people outside of Afghanistan, but certainly makes it a good point to target them in Afghanistan and defines as its primary objective to drive U.S. forces out of the country. It is a major threat to the Afghan State, the Afghan Government, and, frankly, the very political dispensation that has been in the country since 9/11.

Afghanistan remains in a highly precarious position. As the chairman said, the Taliban today is at its strongest point at any point since 9/11. That does not mean that the Taliban does not have problems, does not have shortcomings, or suffer from deficiency and constraints; it does. But nonetheless, its military energy is showing no signs of fizzling out yet.

More significantly, the Taliban is often seen as a less pernicious form of governance than even some of the power brokers associated with the Afghan Government and the post-9/11 dispensation in Afghanistan. And, this is indeed the fundamental problem in the country and the reason why the Taliban still today has so much capacity to regenerate and weather the military pressure from the United States, allies, and even the Afghan security forces. Unless major progress is made in improving governance in Afghanistan and the acceptability and perceptions of governance in Afghanistan, even with beefed-up U.S. forces, we can be exactly in the same predicament 5 or 10 years from now.

The government of National Unity has made some important efforts to improve governance. It has taken on some corruption and criminality but these efforts are hardly sufficient. Much more needs to take place, and the United States must make it a crucial point of its engagement with Afghanistan to insist, facilitate, and help with improving governance.

The priority in improving anti-corruption and anti-crime measures clearly are in the Afghan security and defense forces. Indeed, one of the reasons they have been struggling so much on the battlefield and are taking such large casualties is because of the ethnic and patronage rifts, the corruption that plagues the services that results in poor leadership, poor morale, and a whole host of other enable problems. Clearly, the system of corruption and the system of criminality are an enormous challenge in Afghanistan, defining the very political arrangements of the country.

It is not realistic to expect that everything can be tackled, but even just taking on some steps, particularly before the next Presidential election in Afghanistan, would be very important, once again, starting with the most deleterious forms of corruption and criminality such as rooting out discrimination of entire ethnic groups.

One of the reasons why we saw the fall of Kunduz, the most significant, tactical, and in fact strategic victory of the Taliban so far, is number one along with that—and very much correlated with focusing on the corruption and criminality in the Afghan National Security Forces. There are other measures beyond that that I am glad to answer or speak about during your questions.

[The prepared statement of Ms. Felbab-Brown follows:]

Dr. Vanda Felbab-Brown
Senior Fellow
The Brookings Institution

Subcommittee on Terrorism, Nonproliferation, & Trade
Of the
House Foreign Affairs Committee

Thursday, April 27, 2017
Rayburn 2172
2:00 pm

"Afghanistan's Terrorism Resurgence: Al Qaeda, ISIS, and
Beyond"

Chairman Poe, Ranking Member Keating, and Members of the Subcommittee:

I am honored to have this opportunity to address the Subcommittee on the problem of the resurgence of terrorism in Afghanistan.

The threats posed by terrorism as well as the issues of the country's security, stabilization, and state-building efforts are the domain of my work on Afghanistan, and the subject of my book, *Aspiration and Ambivalence: Strategies and Realities of Counterinsurgency and State Building in Afghanistan* (Brookings, 2013) as well as numerous reports -- most recently "Afghanistan Affectations: How to Break Political-Criminal Alliances during Transitions from War to Peace." I repeatedly conduct fieldwork in Afghanistan on these issues.

In my testimony, I first discuss U.S. interests in Afghanistan. I then analyze the state of Afghanistan today, including the influence of the Taliban and the growth of the Islamic State and the state of the military battlefield and politics in Afghanistan. Third, I examine the sources of militancy and terrorism in Afghanistan, including the role of external sponsors such as Pakistan and crucially, the role of poor governance and extensive predatory criminality and corruption in Afghanistan, and the measures that the Afghan National Unity Government (NUG) of President Ashraf Ghani and CEO Abdullah Abdullah have undertaken to tackle critical challenges. Finally, I end with a set of recommendations.

I conclude that improving governance, not merely beefing up military efforts and countering external sponsors of terrorism in Afghanistan, is critical.

I. U.S. Counterterrorism and Other Interests in Afghanistan

The principal objective of U.S. policy in Afghanistan since the 9-11 attacks has been – and appropriately continues to be -- to ensure that the country does not become a haven for virulent salafi (radical anti-Western jihadi) terrorist groups like al Qaeda. The premise underlying this policy subsequent to the toppling of the Taliban regime in 2001 is that if any part of the liberated territory once again comes under the control of salafi groups or a Taliban sympathetic to such groups, their capacity to increase the lethality and frequency of their terrorist attacks -- including against U.S. assets—will increase since they will be able to use the safe-havens to plan and train for their operations and more easily escape retaliation by the United States and the international community.

Yet there is significant policy and scholarly debate as to how closely aligned the Taliban is today with the terrorist groups and whether the Taliban would once again allow al Qaeda to operate out of a territory it controls. Indeed, some members of the Taliban considered acquiescence to al Qaeda operations a key strategic mistake and call for distancing the group from al Qaeda. The Taliban also actively battles the Islamic State in Afghanistan. At the same time, the Taliban has not denounced al Qaeda officially, undoubtedly because it knows that openly breaking with al Qaeda would cost the Taliban political capital with jihadi groups around the globe and their financial backers, such as in the Middle East.

While al Qaeda has been severely degraded, it has lost none of its zeal to strike Western countries and undermine governments in Asia, the Middle East, and Africa. The group continues to look for opportunities to exploit and territories to colonize, even if only vicariously through proxies, such as in Western and Eastern Africa, even if some of its local alliances are only fleeting and unreliable. In Afghanistan, the terrorist group has also experienced a resurgence in territories where the presence of the Afghan government and international military forces is limited and weak.

The Islamic State in Afghanistan, a newer terrorist group in name, consisting of various Taliban splinter elements and other relabeled militant groups, is also a prime U.S. target.

However, U.S. interests in Afghanistan go beyond terrorism. An unstable Afghanistan risks also destabilizing Pakistan, and as a result, the entire region of Central and South Asia. Pakistan's tribal areas as well as Baluchistan and other areas deep in Pakistan, including Karachi, for example, have been host to many of the salafi groups, and the Afghan Taliban and its vicious Haqqani branch use these areas as safe-havens. Thus Pakistan's cooperation is crucial for effectively countering terrorism in Afghanistan, even if as yet largely not forthcoming. But the reverse is also true: If Afghanistan is unstable and contains salafi groups that leak over into Pakistan, Pakistan itself becomes deeply destabilized and distracted from tackling its other crises, including militancy in the Punjab and a host of domestic calamities, such as intense political contestation, a distorted economy, widespread poverty, and a severe energy crisis.

A disintegration of the Afghan state or an outbreak of a full-blown civil war will be a great boost to salafi groups throughout the world: once again, a great power will be seen as having been defeated by the salafists in Afghanistan. From a strategic *perceptions* standpoint, few areas are as important as Afghanistan. The view that the United States has been defeated does not require that the Taliban retake over the country. From the salafi perspective, merely a gradual, but steady crumbling of the Kabul government, with a progressively greater accretion of territory and power by the Taliban, would be sufficient to claim victory.

Finally, the U.S. reputation and self-regard—as a country that can be relied upon to honor its commitments – are at stake in Afghanistan. In mobilizing support for Operation Enduring Freedom, the mission to topple the Taliban regime in the wake of 9-11, the United States made a pledge to the Afghan people to help them improve their difficult condition and not abandon them once again. Although often caricatured as anti-Western, anti-government, anti-modern, and stuck in medieval times, Afghans crave what others do – relief from violence and insecurity and sufficient economic progress to escape dire, grinding poverty. But on its own, the altruistic concern for the people of Afghanistan is not sufficient for the U.S. to undertake -- or to perpetuate -- what has turned out to be an immensely costly effort. Nor should the tyranny of sunk costs determine U.S. policy in Afghanistan. To paraphrase U.S. strategist George Kennan's counsel to the Senate Committee on Foreign Relations about the U.S. war in Vietnam, the hallmark of a great power is to know when to liquidate unwise commitments. However, U.S. engagement in Afghanistan, including our deployment of adequate military force, still advances key U.S. interests and provides a crucial lifeline for the Afghan government and the country's pluralistic post 9-11 political dispensation. Moreover, once the United States made its initial decision to intervene, consideration for the elemental needs of the Afghan people -- whose lives we have altered so profoundly -- must matter.

Thus, not just counterterrorism objectives but other U.S. interests and values still call for a judicious continuation of U.S. military, political, diplomatic, and economic efforts in Afghanistan.

II. The State of Afghanistan Today

However, Afghanistan remains in a highly precarious condition. After more than a decade of U.S. and international efforts to stabilize Afghanistan and build up the country's governance structures, the U.N. special envoy in Afghanistan Nicholas Haysom stated in March

2016 when briefing the U.N. Security Council that if Afghanistan merely survived 2016 the United Nations mission in the country would consider it a success.[1] Afghanistan did survive 2016 without much of the country falling into the hands of the Taliban, or the government collapsing with a protracted political crisis ensuing, and without a full-blown civil war breaking out. But 2016 also accomplished little in reversing the multiple deleterious trends that motivated the special envoy's comments. Security continued to worsen palpably.

During the two and a half years since the United States and NATO turned the fighting over to the Afghan National Security Forces (ANSF), the Taliban has mounted and sustained its toughest military campaign yet, and the war has become bloodier than ever. Despite the Taliban's internal difficulties, its military energy shows no signs of fizzling out. It has been scoring important tactical and even strategic victories. Insecurity has increased significantly throughout the country, civilian deaths have shot up, and the Afghan security forces are taking large, and potentially unsustainable, casualties as other ANSF deficiencies, including corruption that affects both unit performance and sustainment capacity, persist. Significant portions of Afghanistan's territory, including the provincial capital of Kunduz and multiple districts of Helmand, have fallen (at least temporarily) to the Taliban over the past two years. Moreover, the Islamic State (IS) established itself in Afghanistan in 2015, although it faces multiple and strong countervailing forces.

Although borrowing its name from the Islamic State in the Middle East and proclaiming allegiance to it, the Islamic State in Afghanistan is not a Middle East export to the country. Rather, it consists of several splinter groups and elements expelled from the Taliban, including some too brutal and too sectarian even for the mainstream Taliban. Eastern Nangarhar in particular has emerged as the strongest base of IS presence in Afghanistan. In other parts of the country, such as the north, foreign elements, including Uzbek and Pakistani militants, including factions of Lashkar-e-Taiba and Tehrik-e-Taliban-Pakistan, relabeled themselves IS.

An IS growth in Afghanistan faces substantial obstacles: The group's brutality, greater than even the brutality Afghans have been subjected to for decades, generates resentment. The Taliban has been better able to calibrate brutality and hide or excuse the violence it perpetrates against civilians. At times, the Taliban has even temporarily reduced violence and overly-restrictive edits to generate acceptance by local populations. By contrast, like IS in the Middle East, IS in Afghanistan has chosen to rule by sheer brutality. The Taliban has also sponsored opium poppy cultivation in Afghanistan and the jobs and income it provides for ordinary Afghans, thus generating political capital. IS in Afghanistan, on the other hand, has prohibited opium poppy cultivation both on grounds of ideological purity the strategic goal of ensuring that the only employment available to local men is as IS foot soldiers.

IS in Afghanistan has also drawn the attention of international actors, and the Taliban has been able to capitalize on being seen as a lesser threat by outside powers. For Russia and Iran, the Islamic State is an even greater threat than the Taliban. Both countries have provided support to the Taliban in order to fight IS but also as part of their anti-American efforts.

Far more ominous, however, than the emergence of the Afghan version of IS for the stability of Afghanistan and the long-term success of counterterrorism efforts in the country is how fractious and polarized politics in Afghanistan remain. The National Unity Government (created in the wake of the highly contested presidential elections of 2014) has not yet really

---

[1] Eltaf Najafizada, "If Afghanistan Survives 2016, UN Will Consider It a Success," *Chicago Tribune*, March 17, 2016, http://www.chicagotribune.com/news/sns-wp-blm-afghan-nations-2c8ab8a8-ec23-11e5-a9ce-681055c7a05f-20160317-story.html.

found its feet. The weakness of the NUG, its political dependencies and entanglements, and its other priorities, have also limited and undermined its willingness and ability to robustly tackle the predatory criminality, illicit economies, and organized crime that have become so intermeshed with Afghanistan's political system and international counterinsurgency operations. The country's illicit economies such as illegal mining and logging and drug trafficking have financed and stimulated some aspects of the post-2001 violent conflict. But it is particularly the predatory criminality -- involving usurpation of land, taxes, and customs, generalized extortion, thuggish monopolistic domination of international contracts and local economic markets, and usurpation of international aid – that has even more severely undermined the stabilization and reconstruction efforts. Combined with the capricious and rapacious rule by Afghan powerbrokers, the predatory criminality allows the Taliban, despite its brutality, to to present itself as a more predictable and less corrupt ruler and gives the insurgency critical traction and resilience.

III. The Sources of Militancy and Terrorism in Afghanistan
The persistence of militancy in Afghanistan and the resilience of terrorist groups operating there are the product of external sponsorship as well as weak, corrupt, and inadequate governance in Afghanistan.

The Geopolitics of Afghan Insurgency: Taliban's Sanctuaries in Pakistan
The Taliban developed its military capabilities by taking advantage of sanctuaries in Pakistan's Federally Administered Tribal Areas and the Khyber-Pakhtunkhwa and Baluchistan provinces, and over time even in places far from border areas, such as Karachi. Although nominally a strategic ally of the United States, Pakistan provided the Taliban and its affiliate branches, such as the vicious Haqqani group responsible for the most atrocious terrorist attacks in Afghanistan, including Kabul, with not only safe-havens after 2001, but also direct military and intelligence support. Although receiving very large U.S. counterterrorism assistance in the form of financial aid and military equipment and facing intense U.S. pressure for almost two decades, Pakistan has not severed its support for the Taliban.

A dominant lens though which Pakistan's military-intelligence establishment continues to see Afghanistan is Pakistan's long-standing rivalry with India. More than a decade after 9-11, Pakistan's military-intelligence establishment remains preoccupied with India's ascendance at a time of Pakistan's own stagnation and atrophy. Afghanistan has repeatedly been a prime theater for Indian and Pakistani rivalries. Fearing encirclement by India, Pakistan has been greatly reluctant to suppress Afghan militant groups using Pakistan for sanctuary – such as the Afghan Taliban and Haqqani networks and their insurgent and criminal activities, including many forms of smuggling. Pakistan's continuing support for these groups, despite pressure from the United States and NATO, reflects the persistent view of the Pakistani military-intelligence establishment that the jihadi groups are critical assets in preventing threats on Pakistan's western flank from an India-friendly regime in Kabul and in securing access to Central Asia's trade routes.

However, Pakistan's unwillingness to cease its support for the Taliban also reflects its uncertainties and internal limitations. Pakistan does not have anything approaching total control over the various militant groups that operate from its territory, including the Afghan Taliban. Nor does it have adequate control of the border areas. At the same time, it cannot any longer unequivocally see the Afghan Taliban as an easily-controllable and straight-forward asset. Should the Taliban come to power in Afghanistan or just parts of the country's territory, would it be willing to renege on its debts and friendships with other fellow jihadists, deny bases of operation to anti-Pakistan militant groups, and do Rawalpindi's bidding? Pakistan cannot count on such outcomes. Its policies toward the militants, including its unwillingness for years to launch a military operation into North Warizistan to dislodge the Afghan Taliban there, despite years of intense U.S. pressure, are determined as much by incompetence, inertia, and a lack of capacity, as by calibrated duplicitous misdirection. And when the Pakistan military finally went into North Waziristan in 2014, it allowed the Afghan Taliban and the Haqqanis to escape into Afghanistan, blaming the U.S. and Afghanistan for their inability to secure the border and capture the fleeing insurgents. Indeed, some anti-Pakistani militants also escaped into eastern Afghanistan where the writ of the Afghan state is particularly weak, establishing sanctuaries there.

Finally, Pakistan's willingness to accommodate anti-Afghanistan militant groups is also motivated by fear of provoking them to start violence in Punjab and threaten the core of the Pakistani state, instead of focusing externally.

Weak and Poor Governance and Corruption in Afghanistan

But the Taliban's strength, resilience, and increasing military and political influence are not merely a matter of continued support from Pakistan, nor of the appeal of the Taliban's ideology or anti-Western sentiments or Pashtun mobilization in Afghanistan. In fact, much of the Taliban resilience and growing capacity comes from outperforming the government and government-aligned powerbrokers on the ground in delivery of governance and in the suppression of predatory crime. While Taliban governance is brutal and inadequate and not something most Afghans wish for, they often still find it more tolerable than the misgovernance, power abuse, capriciousness, corruption, and paralysis they face from the state and state-aligned authorities.

A factor that critically allows the Taliban to gain traction with Afghans has been the failure of the post-Taliban regime in Kabul to build up state capacity or deliver good governance and act against predatory criminality. The new state under former President Hamid Karzai (2001-2014) failed not only to meet the expectations of the population for economic development and service delivery but also to maintain elemental security. Karzai sought to govern by cooption and payoffs, such as appointments, to the country's powerbrokers. The current President Ashraf Ghani sought to bring efficiency and technocratic skills to governance, but in doing so reduced the numbers and layers of those having a stake in reform to a much narrower clique of supporters.

Furthermore, the persistent inability to establish good governance, even in areas repeatedly cleared by ISAF and ANSF forces, has often made any security gains highly ephemeral. The state's presence, though meager, often continues to be viewed as basically malign by many Afghans. And it has in fact been characterized by rapaciousness, nepotism, corruption, tribal discrimination, and predatory behavior from government officials and powerbrokers closely aligned with the state. Patronage has been a key determining factor in whether one gets access to resources.

Crime—such as land theft by rival tribes and land grabbing by corrupt power brokers, nepotistic and unfulfilled contracts, and embezzlement—has spread throughout the country. Officers of the Afghan National Police (ANP) have themselves frequently perpetrated various crimes. The police as well as the judicial system are seen by Afghans as among the most corrupt institutions.

The dearth of a multifaceted state presence, including effective law enforcement and formal judicial processes, has exacerbated the pervasive lack of rule of law. Many communities have been left without reliable mechanisms for dispute resolution and the dispensation of justice. At the same time, conflicts over land and water and tribal feuds have escalated due to the absence of the Taliban mailed fist, the lack or venality of formal courts, and a weakening of informal (tribal) dispute resolution codes. Old warlords, now frequently officials at all levels of the Afghan government, have often usurped power for personal enrichment. They regard their positions as governors, police chiefs, and members of provincial development councils (the key governing body at the provincial level), once again, as personal fiefs. During Karzai's presidency, corruption became rampant and deeply embedded. And the corruption has s intensified, partially fueled by the bourgeoning illegal poppy cultivation, but also by the structural deficiencies of state institutions, the predatory behavior of official and unofficial power brokers, and the influx of vast, often unmonitored, sums of foreign aid.

In this environment of uncertainty, pessimism, and unpredictable or absent rule of law, the Taliban has employed several mobilization strategies and messages. It has stepped into the lacuna of good governance by disbursing its own "justice" and order—however harsh and arbitrary—adjudicating disputes, such as over land and water, and acting against crime. For mediating tribal, criminal, and personal disputes, the Taliban does not charge money. Afghans report a great degree of satisfaction with Taliban verdicts, unlike those from the official justice system where they frequently have to pay unaffordable and unreliable bribes. The Taliban also has put a great effort into building a shadow government system that includes its own provincial and district governors and civilian commissions.

No doubt, intimidation by the Taliban and a calculation of who will prevail on the battlefield in any given area also fundamentally determine with whom the population aligns or whether it sits on the fence. If the Afghan government and NATO forces are unable to protect a community from retaliation by the Taliban, and the Taliban specifically targets those seen as cooperating, or even merely interacting with, the Afghan government or ISAF, few will be motivated to risk resistance. Instead, they will passively acquiesce to the Taliban's presence and even to its rule.

The establishment of the National Unity Government emerging from the highly contested and fraudulent 2014 presidential election in Afghanistan provided a unique opportunity to meaningfully improve governance and tackle the criminality and corruption that delegitimized the post-2001 political dispensation. Improving governance and reducing corruption was the one policy on which Ashraf Ghani and Abdullah Abdullah agreed and on which both of them had campaigned.

Instead, although the NUG raised expectations of justice and for an accountable government delivering services and, crucially, combatting corruption and power abuse, it has failed thus far to deliver robustly on any of these promises. One reason is that Ghani and Abdullah were of course deeply beholden to corrupt elites without whose support they would not have been able to run in the elections, and on whose support they continued to depend after the elections. Thus, two and a half years after the formation of the NUG not even one notorious powerbroker has been prosecuted or even dismissed and marginalized. Moreover, immediately after its creation, the NUG was paralyzed by infighting between the two leaders and their factions.

Ghani's unwillingness and inability to move against powerbrokers deeply implicated in criminality and corruption was also driven by his decision early in his administration to prioritize outreach to Pakistan, and through Pakistan to negotiate a peace with the Taliban. Like Karzai, Ghani came to see Pakistan as the magic key to the negotiated deal, and, like Karzai, he became bitterly disappointed by and frustrated with Pakistan in his first two and a half years, with negotiations getting no traction and terrorism and militancy only escalating in Afghanistan and sapping Ghani's political capital.

Thus the anti-crime and anti-corruption measures that Ghani and the NUG did undertake have hardly been robust and momentous enough. Ghani's reopening of the notorious case of the fraudulent Kabul bank did not increase asset recovery and Ghani even sought to make an economic deal with the chief perpetrator of the Kabul bank fraud. With determined international assistance and under international pressure, Ghani's decision to suspend and clean up a $1 billion fuel contract for the Afghan Ministry of Defense was more successful.

However, this important case has not yet translated into a broader clean-up of the massive corruption that still pervades the Afghan security forces, nor has it generated any meaningful follow-up with policies to systematically deter corruption. The tangle of ethnic divisions and rifts and competing patronage networks that for years have run through the Afghan security forces complicate systematic anti-corruption efforts. Challenged on the battlefield and suffering large casualties and retention problems, Afghan security forces are themselves critically weakened and undermined by pervasive corruption and ethnic and patronage rifts. The fall of Kunduz City in October 2016 and the struggle the ANSF have been experiencing in Helmand province for the past two years have provided crucial opportunities to clean up both the most deleterious and debilitating corruption in the ANSF and in local Afghan governance. Neither opportunity has been seized.

Under pressure from donors, the NUG established a specialized anti-corruption court, the so-called Anti-Corruption Justice Center (ACJC) in the run-up to the donors' conference in Brussels in October 2016. However, the ACJC has so far not tried any major cases. Perhaps the most significant anti-corruption and anti-crime accomplishments has been in tax and custom revenue recovery, both of which collapsed in 2014, with theft of revenues vastly surpassing the normal 50 percent theft that characterized the Karzai era. The resulting revenue collection collapse debilitated the Afghan government in 2015, once again highlighting how crucial a more efficient collection of tax and custom revenues is for the functioning of the Afghan state.

In 2015, Afghanistan's government did succeed in delivering a spectacular turnaround in revenue generation: from an eight percent drop in 2014 to a 22 percent rise in 2015.[2] However, such anti-corruption and anti-crime moves have not been anywhere near sufficient to robustly strengthen the functionality of the Afghan government or to reduce the Taliban's anti-crime, anti-corruption, and pro-order narrative. Nor have they helped to reverse the steadily deteriorating security situation in Afghanistan. Indeed, the Taliban, though hardly free of problems, constraints, and limitations, is at its strongest point since 2001,

V. Improving Governance as a Crucial Way Forward

Although most of the trends are problematical, Afghanistan is not on the cusp of defeat. While undermined by corruption and ethnic and patronage rifts and struggling, the Afghan military has not collapsed or ethnically fragmented. The Taliban still does not hold large cities nor does it have anywhere near the territorial control that the Islamic State temporarily achieved in Iraq and Syria. The current Afghan government has adopted many better policies and

[2] William Byrd and M. Khalid Payenda, "Afghanistan's Revenue Turnaround in 2015," Peacebrief No. 201, *USIP*, February 2016, http://www.usip.org/sites/default/files/PB201-Afghanistans_Revenue_Turnaround_In_2015.pdf.

approaches than the previous administration of Hamid Karzai and, as mentioned, managed last year to boost its revenues, a very important development.

Nonetheless, the new U.S. administration, the international community, and the Afghan government must examine what a strategy for an endgame and cessation of violent conflict in Afghanistan entails. The answers today are hardly palatable. One answer is simply hanging on and hoping for the Taliban to self-destruct and wither from within, as a result of the mismanagement of its internal organization, internal fragmentation (perhaps intensified by a U.S. decapitation strategy) or extensive alienation of the Afghan population even in areas where the Afghan government is not liked. The second alternative is hanging on in the hope that the Taliban is willing to negotiate some tolerable power-sharing terms. The two strategies are of course interconnected. The larger problems the Taliban faces on the battlefield -- whether of its own doing or because of ANSF pressure or other insurgent challengers -- the more willing it will be to accept a less ambitious negotiated deal. However, such an inflection point is so far nowhere near, and the Taliban has showed little interest in serious negotiations. Thus the U.S. role in Afghanistan continues to be crucial.

Regardless of whichever pathway for sustainably suppressing Afghan-based terrorism and reducing violent conflict in the country the United States, the international community, and the Afghan government adopt, improving governance in Afghanistan is an indispensable and critical element. Increasing U.S. military presence in Afghanistan is important, but not sufficient.

U.S. long-term goals in Afghanistan over the next decade should include strengthening checks and balances within the Afghan political system, reducing patronage, clientelism, and corruption, and enhancing government service delivery. The steps toward accomplishing these goals include promoting electoral reform, strengthening political parties, and assisting the Afghan parliament and line ministries in developing technical capacity. Many of these policies have already been attempted, often with little meaningful progress.

This does not mean that nothing can be usefully attempted or accomplished within the next two years before the 2019 Afghan presidential elections, for which the Afghan political system is already gearing up. In fact, some ability for the Afghan government incumbents to demonstrate effective governance in anti-crime and anti-corruption measures and transform it into performance-based legitimacy would allow them to reduce their dependence on ethnic and patronage deals for securing votes.

The United States and the international community must work with the Afghan government to reduce corruption and improve governance. They should do so in a prioritized realistic manner: Even taking some modest but sustained steps could make a big difference. That means:

- Tackling first the most dangerous forms of corruption, particularly in the ANSF. This includes rooting out discrimination against entire ethnic and tribal groups that drives local populations into the hands of the Taliban as well as such forms of corruption that altogether paralyze service delivery;

- Reining in predatory criminality and destabilizing warlords one at a time, in a prioritized manner without taking on the entire system and by focusing on the most egregious forms of predatory crime, including extensive land theft, thuggish monopolistic domination of local economic markets, and rape and murder; and

- Continuing to properly sequence counternarcotics efforts with counterterrorism and counterinsurgency, including maintaining a suspension of drug eradication, as eradication drives local populations into the hands of the Taliban.

Good governance is a long-term project, and is, of course, not sufficient. But without evident progress toward it, even beefed-up military efforts will struggle to achieve sustainability and opportunities will remain for terrorist groups to entrench themselves in Afghanistan.

———

Mr. POE. I thank all three of the witnesses. The Chair will re-serve its time until the close of all the questions by the other members, so therefore, I will recognize the ranking member for his 5 minutes.

Mr. KEATING. Thank you, Mr. Chairman. A couple of things, and based on your testimony, I would like to just give you the opportunity to comment on more. Can you give us some of the examples, Doctor, on the criminality and the corruption activities more specifically within the National Security Forces?

Ms. FELBAB-BROWN. The most fundamental problem—I would say—is that positions of leadership at all levels, from unit down to higher-up levels have for years been allotted on the basis of ethnic patronage, very much with mind of rivalries amongst specific commanders, and also related to tribal and ethnic rivalries, but also have been sold out to those who can pay most for the positions. And similar issues, such as getting leave to go to family, has often been associated with those who can pay at the level of individual soldiers. Related to that, with perhaps most significant progress achieved so far, is simply on getting pay down to soldiers as well as getting equipment to soldiers.

Mr. KEATING. Right. Now when I was there a few years ago, they were implementing electronic payments directly, and that was a way to try and ameliorate that. Has that been utilized, first, and has it been successful?

Ms. FELBAB-BROWN. Yes. The process is underway, and it is more linked to biometric systems, one of the primary of sort of focus for the U.S. military and allied military as well as President Ghani. So, progress has been achieved. It is hardly complete; the process is not full. I want to very much compliment the U.S. military in Afghanistan for insisting that only soldiers that are part of the biometric system are paid, because an immense problem has been ghost soldiers that have been receiving payment.

Mr. KEATING. Thank you, Doctor. You gave me some more specifics that I appreciate.

Dr. Jones, you wanted some more time to talk about Pakistan and the regional instability, but also you mentioned Bangladesh. If you could, really comment on Pakistan and Bangladesh and what the effects regionally are there from your vantage point?

Mr. JONES. Sure. My comments on Bangladesh were actually twofold if I had had a little more time. One is that we have seen an increase in Islamic State-Khorasan Province activity, including strikes in and around Bangladesh. We have also seen a growth of al-Qaeda in the Indian Subcontinent of Bangladesh as well.

So we often focus a lot on Afghanistan. The terrorist problem is a regional one, and we often focus also on Pakistan, but Bangladesh has seen a major increase in jihadist activity over the past several years. So, you know, part of the answer here is a much better regional counterterrorism and governance issue than just focusing on Afghanistan or——

Mr. KEATING. Yeah. Would you say in Bangladesh too—with some of the things I have witnessed there in terms of the way their government is running right now—do you think that has been an incubator for this kind of activity or do you think it is just because of geography?

Mr. Jones. Well, I think it is a combination both of geography and also strategy. When Ayman Al-Zawahiri announced the creation of al-Qaeda in the Indian Subcontinent, he specifically asked for Bangladesh to be included in that. So, it was a strategic decision. There is also—and you can see the World Bank or Transparency International data—it is a weak state. It has allowed groups like the ones I mentioned to establish sanctuary there, so again very serious concerns, I think, in Bangladesh.

Mr. Keating. And do any of the witnesses want to talk about what we could do with the Iranian and Russian influence in that area, any suggestions you might have?

Ms. Felbab-Brown. I think it is very important, significant, and laudatory that General Nicholson highlighted the pernicious role of Russia. It is not new. It has been in the making for a number of years even during Russia's nominal cooperation with the United States and Afghanistan. It has been halting and sporadic, and it has clearly disintegrated as part of the difficult U.S.-Russia relationship.

There are no easy fixes, but exposure is an important first step, and there are other ways to engage diplomatically with Russia. Hence, Ranking Member, I emphasize your crucial statements in the beginning about the role of the State Department and the fact that wars cannot simply be won on the military battlefield. The diplomatic effort as well as the——

Mr. Keating. Briefly, on the issue of the Russians supplying arms to the Taliban, is some of that just part of the way they act criminally for their own revenues, criminal syndicates, and things, or do you think it is strategic or both?

Ms. Felbab-Brown. I do believe it is strategic. There is no doubt that the Russian military has dealt with issues of criminal involvement and criminal perpetration, including in the narcotics trade. But I do believe that in the case of supplying weapons to the Taliban it is a very controlled strategic decision and likely indicates rogue members of the Afghan military selling weapons and equipment to the Taliban as well.

I do want to emphasize, however, that support for the Taliban, such as from Iran, in my view, no more than the support that Russia provides, is also very much a function of the regional disbelief, at this point, that a stable, successful government in Afghanistan, as envisioned after 9/11, can be achieved. And it is the tremendous insecurity and uncertainty about what will happen with the government, including as a result of the lack of clarity of U.S. position that encourages——

Mr. Keating. So, we get back to governance too. I know my time is over so I want to yield that back, but we go back to governance again. Thank you.

Mr. Poe. I thank the gentleman. The Chair recognizes the gentleman from California, Colonel Cook, for 5 minutes.

Mr. Cook. Thank you very much, Mr. Chairman.

Continuing the conversation, I wanted to ask how the Chinese view the disturbing role of Russia there, particularly being an ally of—well, China being an ally of Pakistan, and of course, they border Afghanistan. Is that viewed as a major threat any time the

Russians do something along a border that is close to China? And that is up to anyone to address that if they could.

Mr. ROGGIO. Sure, I will address that. I can't speak to what China has or hasn't done with respect to Russian arming of the Taliban, but the Chinese certainly have an interest in stability in Afghanistan. They have economic interests and, obviously, security interests there as well. And there is a group that is based—it is called the Turkistan Islamic Party. It is made up of primarily ethnic Uyghurs from western China and they conduct attacks. They primarily are based in Afghanistan and are closely allied with al-Qaeda as well as the Taliban. They fight inside Afghanistan alongside those groups.

And so you have that bleed-back problem where fighters that come from China to fight inside of Afghanistan come back, and that is a major security issue and security concern for the Chinese Government.

Mr. JONES. If I could just add—I mean—I would say broadly speaking the Chinese have several interests. One is, historically, the economic interest—what I would call soft power. They do have access to a range of mines although they have been slow to develop them because of the security situation. Two, they have been involved in peace negotiations, so trying to bring the Taliban to the peace table, that have not been particularly successful. And three, they have had terrorism concerns. I suspect that anything that would exacerbate their concerns about terrorist activity in the region, including Russian support, would make China somewhat nervous.

Mr. COOK. Doctor?

Ms. FELBAB-BROWN. I agree with those comments, perhaps only to add there is rivalry between China and Russia. It is taking place in Central Asia. The rivalry is, perhaps, not without restraint, but nonetheless that is clearly taking place. So, this is yet another element of the rivalry, the threats, and the interests of China that serve, and Bill articulated also, then implied, that China cannot be happy with Russia's maneuvers toward the Taliban.

Mr. COOK. I want to address the poppy and the drugs that finance the Taliban. And it almost seems counterproductive for the Russians to be supporting the Taliban if you are worried about some of these drugs that would go up through Uzbekistan into Russia, which has had some concerns about growing drug problems of its own. Could you address that drug situation, because it is as I said—it doesn't seem logical.

Ms. FELBAB-BROWN. Sure. I will be very glad to do that. A lot of my expertise is on the issues of drugs, including in Afghanistan. So you are right, Representative Cook, about the poppy being often emphasized as a key interest and problem of Russia. Russia has long blamed the United States for poppy cultivation in Afghanistan, accusing the U.S. of being at best incompetent and often purposeful in allowing poppy cultivation as a tool of poisoning the Russian nation. Obviously, those are outrageous and incorrect claims. The larger issue, of course, is that it is enormously difficult to suppress poppy cultivation, as the Russian Government is well aware, and in fact, any aggressive eradication measures will only feed the Taliban insurgency. The Taliban derives a great deal of support by being able to protect itself—offer itself as a protector of the poppy farmers.

And in fact, one of the reasons why the Islamic State in Nangarhar is so particularly challenged is because it has prohibited poppy cultivation there and essentially mobilized the populations in Achin, Shinwari, Khogyani against itself. However, Russia's interest in countering the drug trade is offset by its other interests, and I would say that Russia's driving interest these days is to be as challenging to the United States across the world as possible.

Mr. Cook. Thank you, I yield back.

Mr. Poe. I thank the gentleman. We are in the process of votes. We do have time for one more series of questions from Ms. Frankel from Florida. That is right.

Ms. Frankel. Thank you. Thank you very much to the panel for being here. So, I guess probably myself, like most Americans, are just very frustrated. My own son has served in the military in Afghanistan as well as USAID, and so I have heard a lot of war stories.

I want to ask you this. Compared to pre-9/11, which obviously led to the catastrophe of the towers, how would you compare Afghanistan and the dangers currently?

Mr. Roggio. Sure; I will tackle that. Well, prior to 9/11, al-Qaeda was operating training camps with no threat of—really, little threat other than maybe an occasional cruise missile strike or something like that, and they were doing it with the support of the Taliban. So, you had the state sponsorship side; as such the Taliban was a state, and they were operating unfettered.

Today, Afghanistan is a war zone. We have American forces there, and they are engaging, targeting, and killing al-Qaeda leaders and trying to prevent them from maintaining safe haven. However, that camp that I mentioned in Shorabak and Kandahar Province that was operating for some time before American—Americans only found out about it when they conducted a raid in Paktika Province several months prior and killed a senior al-Qaeda leader there. Then, they discovered evidence of that camp, and that is when they—and then they spent several months planning the attack.

So, and also I would add that this continuous fighting really serves as a recruiting machine for jihadist groups. That doesn't mean we shouldn't be fighting them there, but the longer we are there fighting the more they are going out and selling their wares. They are getting jihadists to join their cause, be it the Taliban, al-Qaeda, or the myriad of Pakistani jihadist groups operating there. Thank you.

Mr. Jones. If I can add to that, I mean—I think pre-9/11, with al-Qaeda's sanctuary and external plotting and with assistance from the Taliban regime, the threat level to the U.S. was obviously extremely high. Over the next couple of years, it varied somewhat. I mean—I would point to the period of 2009 and 2010 where we had several active plots that went back to that area, Faisal Shahzad in New York City as well as Najibullah Zazi, also New York City plots.

I think today the threat level is serious. I don't see the same number today of external plotting by AQIS, al-Qaeda in the Indian Subcontinent, or core al-Qaeda, but I would say that as we look at future trends, particularly with the return of foreign fighters from Iraq and Syria to the region, it is a serious danger of becoming something like that in the future.

Ms. FRANKEL. So I guess that leads to my next question, which is, does that call for keeping the troops there, more troops? Obviously, I guess the—you have talked about, Doctor, about USAID type efforts, and with the governance and the corruption, I would be curious as to whether you have seen any progress at all in terms of the governance and the corruption issue? But if you could answer both those questions.

Ms. FELBAB-BROWN. I definitely see progress. Clearly, President Ghani is motivated to take on corruption and criminality. He has been constrained, and much more than has been done needs to be done. Unfortunately, more broadly the Afghan political elite continues to be constantly preoccupied and distracted, as mentioned, with politicking and not sufficiently focused on governance, and here is a crucial element of where U.S. policy needs to engage.

If the United States decided to withdraw from Afghanistan, we would be in a situation of full-blown civil war with the Taliban controlling significant territories. No doubt the situation would be dire in the country with serious repercussions for the United States. I do believe that there is good reason to have more troops in Afghanistan, simply because the current force posture does not allow, really, for any meaningful U.S. presence outside of Kabul or even in terms of assistance and eyes on the ground, such as in economic efforts.

However, I also believe that the continuing U.S. engagement—military engagement needs to be coupled with a very explicit political strategy, and I don't mean by the negotiations with the Taliban simply or predominantly, but rather very explicit engagement with the Afghan Government about improving governance. So yes; there is some progress but hardly sufficient, and that needs to be the core of U.S. engagement in the country.

Ms. FRANKEL. Thank you. I think my time, Mr. Chairman. Mr. Roggio, I just want to understand something that you said. You said that fighting begets fighting, and yet I think you are all advocating that we maintain our troops. So, is the theory to try to maintain the troops without fighting or let just as advisers and trainers?

Mr. ROGGIO. Yes. Afghanistan certainly is a catch-22 situation at this time given the length of time we have been there, and I think we have lost the trust of a lot of Afghans. However, I don't see any other option, and I agree with Dr. Brown. If we pull our forces out of there—if we disengage from Afghanistan, it will be largely run by the Taliban, large Taliban pockets in the south, east, north. You will have al-Qaeda back in strength.

So, we have to continue fighting them, and we have to work hard at the governance side as well. We really need to find the right— it is amazing to me that in almost 16 years, we haven't found the right incentives to get the Afghans to do what they need to do to take this fight to the Taliban—to defeat them.

I also agree—negotiations, we have been down this path numerous times. We have been fooled by the Taliban. The Taliban are motivated. Yes; they have their problems militarily and politically, but there is no incentive for them at this point in time. They believe they are winning. They are winning in some areas, and we are not going to get them off the battlefield by negotiating with them. They need to be defeated militarily. We never have done that, and that is going to be extremely difficult until we solve the Pakistan angle, which we have all discussed multiple times here. Thank you.

Mr. POE. I thank the gentlewoman from Florida. The subcommittee will be in recess until 10 minutes after the final vote. There are three votes. Mr. Rohrabacher from California will be the next questioner of the panel.

[Recess.]

Mr. POE. The subcommittee will come to order. The Chair recognizes the gentleman from California, Surfin' Rohrabacher.

Mr. ROHRABACHER. Well, Mr. Chairman, I will have to amend your introduction. It is not the surfing Rohrabacher; it is the suffering Rohrabacher now.

Well, listen, I have enjoyed your testimony today. I am going to have some challenges about some of the positions that you have been advocating. It doesn't mean I don't respect you. I do, because you seem like you are smart and you have done your homework, but I do disagree with you on some things. Also, perhaps, there would be some alternatives that you need to think about that maybe you haven't and, maybe, we haven't as a country. But first let me ask some specific questions on issues. How much heroin and opium is now being produced in Afghanistan?

Ms. FELBAB-BROWN. I do not remember the exact number from last year, but it is a very high number. It is believed to supply at least 90 percent of the world's opiate production.

Mr. ROHRABACHER. Talking about billions of dollars?

Ms. FELBAB-BROWN. Yes, and a significant portion of the country's GDP. So the United Nations Drugs and Crime Office estimates, or used to put out a number—they stopped putting out a number—that only about 4 percent of Afghanistan's GDP is linked to opium poppy. That is a very significant underestimate. They only measured the farm-gate production. I think it is a——

Mr. ROHRABACHER. Okay, so we are talking about billions of dollars that we know is floating around Afghanistan, and is it fair to say that a significant amount of that money gets into the hands of Islamic terrorists including the Taliban? Okay, nobody disagrees with that?

Ms. FELBAB-BROWN. Certainly the Taliban. There has been no evidence that the money has been going to other terrorist groups. It is a significant number of that money that gets to the hands of power brokers linked with the Afghan Government.

Mr. JONES. But the Taliban, which does have relationships with other groups, the Taliban does get a fair amount of money from——

Mr. ROHRABACHER. Okay, so the Taliban gets a fair amount of money and, of course, the Afghan Government, who we put into place—corrupt officials in that group including the family of Mr.

Karzai maybe. We are talking about billions of dollars of wealth. Well, with billions of dollars going like that—coming out like that, I can imagine that would buy a lot of AK-47 bullets, and people wonder where people get the money now.

Do you think we would have the ability—I don't know; are any of you aware that we now have the ability to drop—to spray an area and that within a short period of time, in a way that will not hurt other crops, would eliminate the poppy production in Afghanistan and, basically, would not permit it to grow in that area again for 10 years? Are you aware of that government program?

Okay. Well, let me note for the record, Mr. Chairman, that we have had that capability for at least 20 years and have not touched it and not done it. We didn't do it after 9/11. We had that capability, and we didn't do it. After 9/11, there were storehouses of opium where the Taliban had stored billions of dollars of opium and heroin in special locations in Afghanistan. And I would just go on the record for the first time on this. I notified our Government at the very highest level exactly where those were and that they needed to be bombed because the Taliban needed to be denied that money, and our Government never did that. Our Government never did it. The excuse was always, well, we think it might be too close to a mosque.

All right. In terms of our alternatives now, okay, we ended up bringing Karzai in. We have already heard an assessment of the level of corruption associated with the Karzai regime and the Karzai family. We created that. Those of us who were engaged with this effort before that time wanted the king to return the king. He was the one guy, Pashtun and the rest of them, who everybody respected. Instead, we brought in Karzai, who it appears as being said today oversaw massive corruption.

But now, back to how we now are in. So now, we are in a bad spot.

We didn't do what was right then, and now we are in a bad spot.

And let me just say for the record, Mr. Chairman, that the alternative is not just putting more U.S. troops into Afghanistan.

And let me ask the question of our panel, do you know how many U.S. troops were in Afghanistan after 9/11 at the time when the Taliban were driven out of Kabul? Do we know? Two hundred. Two hundred. So, obviously, 200 Americans weren't the ones who drove them out, it was the Northern Alliance. And instead of having a government in which we respected these individual leaders and a decentralist approach—have any of you read the Afghan Constitution? Have you read the—okay.

Who in the Afghan Constitution, who appoints the local police? Kabul. Who appoints the local educators? Kabul. We gave them, Mr. Chairman, the most centralized government plan for the people who are the most decentralized culture in the world, and now they are upset, and they are willing to go along with any number of groups.

And I am going to leave it with this one thought, because I am sorry if I am taking too much time, Mr. Chairman. The Flying Tigers came in, and really, they were private people, and they were saving Chiang Kai-shek from this onslaught of the Japanese before Pearl Harbor. They were actually on the way there. Their first mis-

48

sion actually happened a couple days after Pearl Harbor, but they
were on their way over to create an air force.

We need air cover; do we not, sir? Do not our friends in Afghanistan need the air cover? It is now being proposed by a private sector of folks, who are not dissimilar from the Flying Tigers, that
they would go to Afghanistan and provide this service. And I would
hope that anybody reading this testimony understands that we
don't need to send massive troops in when private sector people
will get the job done or if people in their own country would get
it done. Thank you very much, Mr. Chairman.

Mr. POE. I thank the gentleman. The Chair recognizes the
gentlelady from California, Ms. Torres.

Ms. TORRES. Thank you, Mr. Chairman, and thank you to the
panel for taking time to be here today.

Based on recent statements by General Nicholson and Secretary
Mattis, it appears increasingly clear that Russia has been arming
the Taliban. What is your assessment of Russian intentions in Afghanistan? And I would like to hear an opinion from maybe the
three of you. How do you think the United States should respond
to Russia's intervention in Afghanistan?

Mr. ROGGIO. Sure. I believe Russia's intentions are primarily focused on targeting the growing threat of the Islamic State. What
used to be al-Qaeda's branch in the Caucasus has now become part
of the Islamic State, and there is a threat also that emanates from
the region from the Islamic State. They are concerned about that
in the Central Asian countries, which are in Russian sphere of influence as well as attacks in their country.

So, I think part of that is an attempt. Because the Taliban and
the Islamic State are enemies, they do fight each other. Although
this was more common a year or 2 ago, they have sort of, kind of
come to some uneasy truce. I believe that they are also—I think
this is also a ploy by the Russians to gain influence with the
Taliban as well as, you know, as possibly a little payback for
United States efforts in Afghanistan in the 1980s.

As far as what the United States can do about this, I think there
is only really political pressure that can be applied. As far as Russian support for the Taliban, it is pretty low on the chain. When
you look at it, you know, you have the primary state sponsor for
the Taliban and jihadist groups in Pakistan is—or in Afghanistan
is Pakistan, and I would even say Iran poses a bigger threat with
its support for the Taliban as well.

Russia; they are providing light arms as far as I could tell at this
point in time. We haven't had a lot of specifics of what that Russian support is, but really the only solution is diplomatic here. We
are not going to go to war with the Russians for providing a small
amount of arms to the Taliban.

Ms. TORRES. Thank you.

Mr. JONES. I would say, based on my look at this, there are at
least three potential motivations for Russia right now. One, I think
if we look broadly at Russian operations in Syria, even Russian
presence in Libya as well as in Afghanistan and other locations,
they are expanding and attempting to expand their influence as
part of a resurgence effort. Second, I think they are concerned
about the Islamic State and other groups operating in Afghanistan,

particularly ones that may come back from Iraq and Syria into Central Asia, the Caucasus, and South Asia. And third, they have had some concerns about the U.S. withdrawal from the regions and what gets left on their southern flank.

I mean, I think there are a few things that the U.S. can do. One is—I mean—to continue to target, as the U.S. has, the Islamic State in the region including in Afghanistan. I mean, it is a threat so I think there is some reason for the Russians to be concerned about ISIS there. I think the U.S. should stop saying, as it has done at various points over the last couple of years, that it is going to leave.

I think that may be helpful so the Russians realize we are not leaving for the foreseeable future; it is a conditions based effort. And I think, and Vanda said this earlier, that we should be as transparent as possible on what they are doing so we have evidence to show it publicly.

Ms. TORRES. Thank you. Dr. Brown?

Ms. FELBAB-BROWN. I agree with the three stated motivations. Russia's official justification for its engagement and not denial of support for the Taliban has been that the Islamic State is a bigger threat for them. I think that is the calculation. I don't think that is the sole calculation, however. I do believe that Russia, like other regional actors, are uncertain about the outcome and are hedging and cultivating proxies. It is not simply the Taliban that Russia is engaging, but also other proxies that have been not violently, but in political opposition to Kabul.

So, it is a wide range of actors that Russia is engaging just as Iran is engaging, and clearly, they have now moved to directly military cultivating the Taliban. And I do believe that Russia defines its primary strategic objective as challenging the United States across the world. They waited in Afghanistan to challenge the United States, but they never wholeheartedly supported U.S. efforts in Afghanistan, and now they determined that this is yet another theater where they can engage.

I do believe that the primary response is one of diplomatic exposure and diplomatic engagement and, perhaps, diplomatic isolation of Russia. However, there are other interdiction options also not of Russian agents in the Taliban, but certainly of some of the proxies that Russia is engaging with, that does not necessarily mean military eliminating them; but perhaps, blowing up the heroin stockpiles that the representative mentioned that belong to proxies and favored power brokers of Russia in Afghanistan as a tool, as a signal.

Ms. TORRES. Thank you, and my time is up. I yield back.

Mr. POE. I thank the gentlelady. The Chair recognizes the gentleman from Illinois Mr. Schneider.

Mr. SCHNEIDER. Thank you, Chairman Poe. Thank you to you and the ranking member for calling this hearing, and I want to thank the witnesses for sharing with us your perspectives. This is obviously, as you have stated, a very complex issue. Before I continue, I also want to join with my colleagues in extending my personal and our condolences to the families of the fallen fighters in Afghanistan. Our thoughts and prayers are with them.

So Mr. Roggio, and I mentioned this to you on the break. You mentioned something called the Long War and that could be looking backward. We have been in Afghanistan now approaching its 16th year, or it could be looking forward. From your perspective what are we looking at going forward as far as the time of our involvement here?

Mr. ROGGIO. Yes, this long war has expanded greatly since 9/11. If we look at just the threat of al-Qaeda, it was operating in Afghanistan alongside the Taliban fighting the Northern Alliance, running training camps, and then it had a small presence in a couple of countries throughout the world operating on a cellular level.

Since particularly with the Arab Spring, the jihadist threat has expanded greatly. We now have active war zones in Syria, Iraq, Yemen, Somalia, Mali, Libya, Afghanistan, Pakistan, and Southeast Asia. We could go on listing the countries where we have active jihadist insurgencies. We have had attacks here in the homeland, attacks in Europe. The reality is we are fighting this enemy militarily, but we are not tackling their ideology, which to me is the prime driver of these Islamist militant groups.

Until we and our allies come up with a way to discredit them, to discredit their ideology, we are just not killing them fast enough. We have great success in killing terrorist leaders, in killing fighters in drone strikes, and that has been fine. But they have shown a remarkable capability to replace their leadership and that is the way they have been expanding their operations.

Mr. SCHNEIDER. And I am sorry just because of time—and they are resilient. But if I can turn to Dr. Jones, I think it was you that said this. If not, I apologize. I may have lost it while we had stepped away. But you indicated that our policy across administrations has been, I think the term you used was, a mess. And my——

Mr. JONES. Bill may have used that.

Mr. SCHNEIDER. All right. That is just—I may have gotten it right. But my question, this is for the whole panel, is as we look at the policy as it is today with the challenges—and Mr. Roggio you talked about how quickly, how resilient they are and how quickly they have expanded and can pop up with new members, new resources—as we try to put a policy into place that has a sense of order, what does that order look like? What specific goals would you apply? What would be the timelines we should be considering as we look at policy here from our position?

Mr. JONES. Sure, I have a couple of comments on that. I mean, I think as I have looked at this and I have been involved myself in this as a civilian and in the military in Afghanistan, I think our objectives at this point should be fairly limited. We are dealing with a government that has challenges and is relatively weak, but I would set up several objectives. One is to prevent the Taliban from overthrowing the government and from holding urban terrain, you know, major urban terrain, and I think that is potentially doable.

I think we should continue to target groups that are plotting attacks against the U.S. both here and overseas, and I think we should continue to support the government and local actors as well on the ground. I don't know the timelines there. I think those are in American interests. I think one can do those with a limited presence on the ground with both diplomatic, development, and military.

51

But I think that is a condition based approach rather than a timeline, and I think as long as we are moving in those directions and the government is relatively competent, I would personally support that.

Mr. SCHNEIDER. Dr. Felbab-Brown, your perspective? You bring experience beyond just this region; across the globe. What do you see as some of the objectives, challenges, and metrics that we can measure progress by?

Ms. FELBAB-BROWN. Beyond the unfortunate position of not having a good alternative to persevering, we can decide to liquidate the mission in Afghanistan, and indeed, to quote a prominent U.S. strategist or paraphrase, the hallmark of a wise power is to know when to liquidate unwise commitments.

I don't believe we have reached that stage in Afghanistan. Our perseverance still keeps the country from outright civil war and the Taliban from toppling the regime and holding significant territories. Those are very important means to achieving or to maintaining U.S. objectives.

I would think about the conditions under which the U.S. support would no longer be maintaining those objectives such as if the Afghan military turned on itself, if there were massive defections, if in fact political infighting started in advance of the Presidential 2019 elections. Those would be markers for me to reconsider liqui-dating despite the terrible cost to U.S. counterterrorism objectives.

Until then, I do believe that we need to persevere, perhaps, with a boosted military presence as well. However, the perseverance and the military presence cannot be decoupled from strong focus and governance. We need to change the perceptions of the Afghan people where the Taliban is really not so much worse than the predatory rule of local power brokers or even Afghan officials associated with the government.

Mr. SCHNEIDER. Thank you. My time is up. As with all complex issues but especially here, the answers to a question leads to so many more questions. I wish we had more time, but thank you for being here.

Mr. POE. And the gentleman can submit those questions for the record and we will make sure that the witnesses invite those, or answer those questions in a timely manner; not take 16 years to answer them for us. I will recognize myself, as I mentioned, as last to ask questions. I want to read a statement made by the Ambassador from Afghanistan to the United Nations—only portions of it.

In recent months, dozens of terrorist attacks across Afghanistan have claimed scores of innocent lives. The Taliban has claimed responsibility for most of these attacks, but regardless of whose names are being labeled on these attacks, our own investigations have clearly established that they were generally plotted beyond our frontiers on the other side of the Durand line, mainly Pakistan. Mr. President, it is a fundamental factor which needs to be addressed.

So I want to address that with the remaining time that we have. Dr. Jones, I will ask you first. Explain, as you can concisely, what Pakistan's mischief is regarding terrorist groups that are related to Pakistan, hide in Pakistan, and they go to Afghanistan. Explain that relationship if you can.

Mr. JONES. Sure. I think this in part comes down to what I would call the great power of politics, meaning Afghanistan sits— and Pakistan is a major border with Afghanistan. Afghanistan's strongest regional ally is India. That is unacceptable to Pakistan; India is an enemy. So while the Afghan Government has an ally in the Indian Government, Pakistan has resorted to proxy organizations to further its foreign policy goals both in places like Jammu and Kashmir against the Indians and in Afghanistan and that means support to organizations like the Haqqani Network and the Taliban. So it is a proxy war.

Mr. POE. Either one of our other witnesses want to weigh in on this?

Mr. ROGGIO. I would agree with Dr. Jones. The Pakistani Government is, you know, continuing with its policy or its strategy of strategic depth. It views everything through the lens of fighting India. And unfortunately, some of these jihadist groups that have spawned from the Pakistani efforts to fight India to establish strategic depth in Afghanistan. It has come back to bite them with groups like the movement of the Taliban in Pakistan and other groups which have attacked the Pakistani State. And unfortunately, Pakistan seems unwilling to recognize this.

It is still—while it fights the movement of the Taliban in Pakistan, it continues to support other groups like Lashkar-e-Taiba and host of other groups, because they are willing to serve as Pakistan's strategic depth. Until the Pakistani Government, leaders and military intelligence—until they come to grips with this, this problem is going to exist for decades.

Mr. POE. Would you agree that with the statement of Admiral Mullen in 2011 that the Haqqani Network acts as a veritable arm of Pakistan's Inter-Service Intelligence agency?

Mr. ROGGIO. Yes, I absolutely would agree. And keep in mind the operational leader of the Haqqani Network, Siraj Haqqani. He is also one of two deputy emirs for the Taliban. The Haqqani Network, they will tell you—their propaganda has said look, we don't exist, there is no Haqqani Network. We are the Taliban. That is both true and untrue. It is a subset of the Taliban. Its leaders are integrated with the Taliban, so it is a major; it is receiving major support from the Pakistani Government and, you know, they are killing Americans. And we have to—we really need to figure out a way to get Pakistan to stop supporting the Taliban.

Mr. POE. And in recent years, the United States has given over $33 billion in some form of aid to Pakistan. Pakistan directly or indirectly supports the Haqqani Network in theory. That network, as we mentioned earlier, has killed more Americans in the region than any other terrorist group. To me that is something that we should not accept. We should not accept sending money to a country that supports a terrorist group that kills Americans. I think there is a real problem with that.

Dr. Jones, do you want to weigh in on that?

Mr. JONES. No. I think it is a serious problem. I mean, I have been on the receiving end of it myself. I have lost friends and colleagues because of Haqqani Network attacks. I think it is a very, very serious problem. I would support, as the U.S. did last year, when it has a strike against a Taliban leader as it did with Mullah

Mansour to take that strike. I mean, I think it is worth considering the costs and benefits, but I would applaud the administration for targeting the Taliban leader last year.

Mr. POE. All right, I will yield back the remainder of my time. I want to thank all of our witnesses for being here. I certainly want to thank the members of the committee. This has not been an encouraging hearing about the 16-year war that is taking place, but I appreciate you being here. Maybe we can figure out some solutions for what Congress' role should be and advise the administration as well. This subcommittee is adjourned.

[Whereupon, at 4:14 p.m., the subcommittee was adjourned.]

APPENDIX

MATERIAL SUBMITTED FOR THE RECORD

56

SUBCOMMITTEE HEARING NOTICE
COMMITTEE ON FOREIGN AFFAIRS
U.S. HOUSE OF REPRESENTATIVES
WASHINGTON, DC 20515-6128

Subcommittee on Terrorism, Nonproliferation, and Trade
Ted Poe (R-TX), Chairman

TO: MEMBERS OF THE COMMITTEE ON FOREIGN AFFAIRS

You are respectfully requested to attend an OPEN hearing of the Committee on Foreign Affairs, to be held by the Subcommittee on Terrorism, Nonproliferation, and Trade in Room 2172 of the Rayburn House Office Building (and available live on the Committee website at http://www.ForeignAffairs.house.gov):

DATE: Thursday, April 27, 2017

TIME: 2:00 p.m.

SUBJECT: Afghanistan's Terrorist Resurgence: Al-Qaeda, ISIS, and Beyond

WITNESSES: Mr. Bill Roggio
Editor
Long War Journal
Foundation for Defense of Democracies

Seth G. Jones, Ph.D.
Director
International Security and Defense Policy Center
RAND Corporation

Vanda Felbab-Brown, Ph.D.
Senior Fellow
Center for 21st Century Security and Intelligence
Foreign Policy Program
The Brookings Institution

By Direction of the Chairman

The Committee on Foreign Affairs seeks to make its facilities accessible to persons with disabilities. If you are in need of special accommodations, please call 202/225-5021 at least four business days in advance of the event, whenever practicable. Questions with regard to special accommodations in general (including availability of Committee materials in alternative formats and assistive listening devices) may be directed to the Committee.

COMMITTEE ON FOREIGN AFFAIRS

MINUTES OF SUBCOMMITTEE ON _____ *Terrorism, Nonproliferation, and Trade* _____ HEARING

Day___ *Thursday*___ Date_____ *April 27, 2017*___ Room_____ *2172*_____

Starting Time ___ *2:25p.m.*___ Ending Time ___ *4:14 p.m.*___

Recesses ___ *I*___ (*3:12 pm* to *3:48pm*) (____to____) (____to____) (____to____) (____to____) (____to____)

Presiding Member(s)
Chairman Ted Poe

Check all of the following that apply:

Open Session ☑
Executive (closed) Session ☐
Televised ☑

Electronically Recorded (taped) ☑
Stenographic Record ☑

TITLE OF HEARING:

"Afghanistan's Terrorist Resurgence: Al-Qaeda, ISIS, and Beyond"

SUBCOMMITTEE MEMBERS PRESENT:

Reps. Poe, Keating, Frankel, Cook, Titus, Perry, Torres, Zeldin, Schneider

NON-SUBCOMMITTEE MEMBERS PRESENT: *(Mark with an * if they are not members of full committee.)*

Rohrabacher

HEARING WITNESSES: Same as meeting notice attached? Yes ☑ No ☐
(If "no", please list below and include title, agency, department, or organization.)

STATEMENTS FOR THE RECORD: *(List any statements submitted for the record.)*

SFR - "United Nations Security Council Debate on the Situation in Afghanistan Statement By H.E. Mahmoud Saikal - Ambassador, Permanent Representative of the Islamic Republic of Afghanistan to the United Nations" submitted by Chairman Ted Poe

TIME SCHEDULED TO RECONVENE _____
or
TIME ADJOURNED ___ *4:14 p.m.*___

Subcommittee Staff Associate

MATERIAL SUBMITTED FOR THE RECORD BY THE HONORABLE TED POE, A REPRESENTA-
TIVE IN CONGRESS FROM THE STATE OF TEXAS, AND CHAIRMAN, SUBCOMMITTEE ON
TERRORISM, NONPROLIFERATION, AND TRADE

United Nations Security Council Debate on the Situation in Afghanistan

STATEMENT BY

H.E. Mahmoud Saikal

Ambassador, Permanent Representative of the Islamic Republic of Afghanistan to the United Nations

Security Council Debate on the Situation in Afghanistan

10 March 2017

NEW YORK

(check against delivery)

بسم الله الرحمن الرحيم

Thank you Mr. President. Let me congratulate the United Kingdom on its leadership of the Council this
month. I thank the Secretary General, Antonio Guterres, for presenting his first report on the situation in
Afghanistan. Also, allow me to thank the SRSG, Ambassador Tadamichi Yamamoto, and Afghanistan's
Independent Human Rights Commissioner, Dr. Sima Samar, for their briefings.

Given the severity of the situation in my country, I would like to dedicate my statement today to the
challenging security situation, hidden agendas, the peace process and the ever-increasing necessity for
regional and global cooperation.

Mr. President,

In recent months, dozens of terrorist attacks across Afghanistan have claimed scores of innocent lives. In
January, three simultaneous terrorist attacks in Kabul, Kandahar, and Helmand provinces killed and
maimed over 160, including six UAE diplomats. In February, the Supreme Court, our symbol of justice,
was attacked, causing numerous fatalities. Last week, two separate attacks in the heart of Kabul killed
many civilians. Finally, just two days ago Afghanistan's largest hospital was attacked, leaving over 140
killed and wounded, many of whom were doctors, nurses, and patients. The Taliban have claimed
responsibility for most of these attacks, but regardless of whose names are being labeled on these
attacks, our own investigations have clearly established that they were generally plotted beyond our
frontiers, on the other side of the Durand Line. This, Mr. President, is the fundamental factor which
needs to be addressed.

The UN Security Council issued prompt statements condemning these attacks in strongest terms, for
which we are thankful. The statements underlined – and I quote: "the need to bring perpetrators,
organizers, financiers and sponsors of these reprehensible acts of terrorism to justice". It also urged "all
States, in accordance with their obligations under international law and relevant Security Council
resolutions, to cooperate actively with the Afghan authorities in this regard." This is indeed what
Afghanistan has been asking for many years. My Government and people would like to know why, after

countless terrorist atrocities and specific Security Council statements condemning them, we are still witness to impunity for perpetrators and orchestrators of endless violence?

Mr. President,

Let me be very clear. The conflict in our country is not homegrown, as some desperately and deceptively try to portray. On the contrary, it is the nexus of illicit narcotics, violent extremism, and state sponsorship of terrorism with regional dimensions and global consequences. Tragically, it has morphed into an undeclared war by a neighboring state that has for many years, and still continues to coordinate, facilitate, and orchestrate violence through proxy forces and more than 20 terrorist networks. These groups benefit from a full-fledged external infrastructure to keep Afghanistan off-balance for motives that are inconsistent with our desire to live in a peaceful and prospering region.

In earlier statements to this Council, we have emphasized, time and again, on Pakistani actions that sustain terrorist activities in our country. Today, let me quote leading Pakistani officials themselves. General Pervez Musharraf, who led Pakistan for eight years as President, proudly commented in a 2015 interview with The Guardian newspaper that "Pakistan's Inter Services Intelligence (ISI) had given birth to the Taliban to counter Indian action against Pakistan". Last year, Mr. Sartaj Aziz, Pakistan Prime Minister's Adviser on Foreign Affairs, went on record to say that Taliban leaders reside in Pakistan and that they have influence over them. A couple of weeks ago, Mr. Ashraf Jehangir Qazi, former ambassador of Pakistan to the US, Russia, China, and India and UN SRSG to Iraq and Sudan, wrote in the Herald Magazine of Pakistan: "after the Soviet defeat and withdrawal, we (wittingly or unwittingly) unleashed a ruinous civil war and imposed a barbaric and medieval Taliban upon the hapless Afghan people." His words are but confirmation of the truth that "Pakistan talks one policy, but walks the other". Mr. Husain Haqqani, another former Ambassador of Pakistan to the US and Sri Lanka, categorizes in clear terms, in a NYT 2013 article, the links between Pakistan's state apparatus and the Taliban over time, and mentions in the context of peace talks that "the Taliban and their Pakistani mentors have hardly changed their arguments or their tendency to fudge facts". These quotes and admissions that I just read were not "rhetoric from Kabul" or "blame game" as often claimed by a known member state. This was Pakistan talking!

Mr. President,

Against this backdrop, in February, a series of unfortunate terrorist attacks in Pakistan killed dozens and wounded many more innocent men, women, and children. As is the case, Afghans always share the pain and anguish of our Pakistani brothers and sisters. However, the Government of Pakistan, immediately and without any regard for an investigative process or clear facts, blamed Afghanistan for the attacks and resorted to increased breaches of our territorial integrity, the closing of the main border crossings, blockading trade and transit, and harassing our nationals traveling to or living in their country. Such measures constitute a clear violation of principles of WTO and the rights of land locked countries, including their access to sea.

From January till today, we recorded at least 59 instances of violations of Afghan territory by Pakistan military forces, including three violations of our air space, over 1375 cross-frontier artillery shellings that caused dozens of casualties, displacement of 450 families in the middle of cold winter in our eastern provinces, burning of our forests, illegal construction of infrastructure near the frontier region, and hostile maneuvering of tanks and heavy weaponry.

The travesty of decorum in neighborly relations did not cease there, as the familiar pattern of obfuscation of facts and diversionary tactics took over. We were then issued by the Government of Pakistan a list of, so-called, 76 suspected terrorists in Afghanistan, which after close inspection by us and our international partners, was found to be in desperate need of verification.

Our reaction to all these provocations has been sober and methodical. We have submitted 25 protest notes to the Government of Pakistan and, in the past few weeks, summoned their ambassador to Kabul on three occasions. We have submitted to their Government a list of 86 known terrorists and 32 Taliban training centers, including Haqqani network centers, asking for their immediate closure. We have asked for a third-party verification of the two sides' efforts. No response has yet been received. The UN Secretary General, this noble Council, and other international partners are all appraised of these developments.

Mr. President,

While terrorist attacks in Pakistan are strongly deplored by our Government, we are surely witnessing the blowback effects of using violent proxies as instruments of foreign policy, which was adopted by decision-making circles in that country in the 1980s, and is still being pursued to this day. In other words, the chickens are coming home to roost! We have reminded our Pakistani counterparts on many occasions that "you reap what you sow". We say once again, it is time to change that failed policy for your own sake, desist from using radical terrorists as a foreign policy accessory, and genuinely join the international fight against all forms and shades of terrorism.

By bleeding Afghanistan, Pakistan is not only trying to create a stalemate on the battlefield, but it is also hindering the political track. Hoping to gain legitimacy for groups such as the Taliban, Pakistani decision-makers continue to use "plausible deniability" and shifting blame, as part of their defensive tactics while manipulating geo-political fault lines to their advantage.

They forget that legitimacy in my country flows through the people and a constitutional order, not through acts of terror, intimidation, and forced imposition of extremist thinking and radical behavior by misinterpreting and misusing our sacred religion of Islam.

Talks leading to a peace process can only succeed when policy is revised, the use of sanctuaries is prohibited, terrorist financing is curbed, and violence is renounced. Peace cannot be achieved by paying lip service and pretending to be a selective victim.

Mr. President,

As we speak, the Afghanistan National Defense and Security Forces (ANDSF) are battling, with great resilience and determination, a network of regional and global terrorist groups, who have come to Afghanistan for various objectives. In 2016, our forces prevented the Taliban and terrorist affiliates to capture major population centers. In January, we adopted a four year National Security Strategy, which focuses on bolstering combat capabilities, leadership development, and improving unity and coordination of command. The fight against terrorism will continue with even greater resolve, on the basis of our security strategy. That said, continued support from our international partners remains critical for the sustainability of our forces over the long haul. In that light, I wish to reiterate, here again, that Afghanistan's strategic partnerships will, in no way, serve a detriment to any country within our region or beyond. On the contrary, investments in Afghanistan's security are in fact an investment in regional and global security.

Mr. President,

For years, the lack of a meaningful and result-oriented channel of dialogue aimed at addressing root causes of tension between Kabul and Islamabad has created a huge trust deficit. Reducing this deficit requires political will and healthy interactions between our two countries. On our part, if we look at the record, Afghanistan has always been ready to engage in constructive and result-oriented dialogue.

We welcome any earnest and transparent initiative to help us reach that stage of dialogue. In our view, the Quadrilateral Coordination Group (QCG) and the recent six-party Moscow conference on Afghanistan can serve useful in that endeavor, if utilized and coordinated properly. These initiatives, among others, emphasize a set of guiding principles, most notably that any peace process should be Afghan-led and that the region must support the Afghan Government in its quest for sustainable peace. Moreover, they also recognize the importance of having all relevant regional and global actors on board in a constructive manner.

We know from previous experience that any prospect of success in peace efforts rests on a number of important principles:

(1) Any attempt at resolving current and/or historic issues between governments require strong national political will and an impartial and agreed upon international arbitrator in good standing;

(2) All sides need to define and agree on the scope of dialogue and negotiations, leading to a specific set of deliverables and outcomes that can be supported by regional stakeholders, and eventually guaranteed by the international community;

(3) All sides need to be willing to address the root causes of conflict, not its by-products, and resolve areas of contention by adhering to and making use of international law, pragmatic precedence, and/or other best practice and judicial norms, and void of presumed realpolitik assumptions;

(4) Given Afghanistan's sensitive geopolitical position, all peace-building and anti-terrorism efforts, in the long-run, need to have all key stakeholders on board, take the complexities of an evolving regional and global security architecture into account, and agree to a status that assures stability, balance, non-interference, sovereignty, and positive engagement in Afghanistan; and

(5) Keeping principles of sovereignty and non-interference central to our objectives, this requires Afghanistan to turn into a symbol of international cooperation, where global and regional powers set

aside their rivalries and short-term interests, by agreeing to cooperate in a spirit of confidence for long-term mutual benefit.

Mr. President,

Finally, in a few days we will celebrate Nowruz – start of our New Year and the first day of Spring – a festive occasion that symbolizes peace, solidarity, and togetherness among our people and the wider region at-large. But as recent attacks have shown, Afghans will celebrate with a heavy heart. On the other hand, with their planned so-called spring offensive, the Taliban and other terrorist groups are adamantly focused on producing more horror, panic, and fear, leaving little room for joy among our men, women, and children.

This time, we hope to collectively counter their new season of murder and mayhem. Our brave and courageous national security forces are ready and highly determined to defend our people with full confidence and strength. We survived the post-transition 2015; we countered and defeated every major plan of the terrorist groups and their foreign backers to capture and control main population centers in 2016; and in 2017, we will, with your support, and by the Grace of God Almighty, humiliate and destroy the enemies of peace and security in Afghanistan. We are fully committed to making sure that our New Year will be one in which we will open the way for durable peace in our country, our region, and around the world. We join Secretary-General Antonio Guterres in his appeal to the international community for making 2017 a year of peace. For us, it starts at home.

Thank You Mr. President.